International Dimensions of Corporate Finance

PRENTICE-HALL FOUNDATIONS OF FINANCE SERIES

Herbert E. Dougall
Capital Markets and Institutions

Edwin J. Elton and Martin J. Gruber
Finance as a Dynamic Process

Jack Clark Francis and Stephen H. Archer
Portfolio Analysis

George H. Hempel and Jess B. Yawitz
Financial Management of Financial Institutions

Robert K. Jaedicke and Robert T. Sprouse
Accounting Flows: Income, Funds, and Cash

Baruch Lev
Financial Statement Analysis: A New Approach

Dileep R. Mehta
Working Capital Management

James T. S. Porterfield
Investment Decisions and Capital Costs

David A. Ricks
International Dimensions of Corporate Finance

Alexander A. Robichek and Stewart C. Myers
Optimal Financing Decisions

James C. Van Horne
Function and Analysis of Capital Market Rates

J. Fred Weston
The Scope and Methodology of Finance

PRENTICE-HALL FOUNDATIONS OF FINANCE SERIES

Ezra Solomon, *Editor*

International Dimensions of Corporate Finance

David A. Ricks

Faculty of Finance
Ohio State University

PRENTICE-HALL, INC., Englewood Cliffs, New Jersey 07632

201- 555-1212

(201)- 592-2000

Library of Congress Cataloging in Publication Data

RICKS, DAVID A (date)
International dimensions of corporate finance.

(Prentice-Hall foundations of finance series)
Includes bibliographies and index.
1.–International business enterprises–Finance.
2.–Corporations–Finance. I.–Title.
HG4028.I53R5 658.1'5 77-22693
ISBN 0-13-471714-7
ISBN 0-13-471706-6 pbk.

Printed in the United States of America

10 9 8 7 6 5 4 3 2 1

PRENTICE-HALL INTERNATIONAL, INC., *London*
PRENTICE-HALL OF AUSTRALIA PTY. LIMITED, *Sydney*
PRENTICE-HALL OF CANADA, LTD., *Toronto*
PRENTICE-HALL OF INDIA PRIVATE LIMITED, *New Delhi*
PRENTICE-HALL OF JAPAN, INC., *Tokyo*
PRENTICE-HALL OF SOUTHEAST ASIA PTE. LTD., *Singapore*
WHITEHALL BOOKS LIMITED, *Wellington, New Zealand*

TO

Lesley

Editor's Note

The subject matter of financial management is in the process of rapid change. A growing analytical content, virtually nonexistent ten years ago, has displaced the earlier descriptive treatment as the center of emphasis in the field.

These developments have created problems for both teachers and students. On the one hand, recent and current thinking, which is addressed to basic questions that cut across traditional divisions of the subject matter, do not fit neatly into the older structure of academic courses and texts in corporate finance. On the other hand, the new developments have not yet stabilized and as a result have not yet reached the degree of certainty, lucidity, and freedom from controversy that would permit all of them to be captured within a single, straightforward treatment at the textbook level. Indeed, given the present rate of change, it will be years before such a development can be expected.

One solution to the problem, which the present Foundations of Finance Series tries to provide, is to cover the major components of the subject through short independent studies. These individual essays provide a vehicle through which the writer can concentrate on a single sequence of ideas and thus communicate some of the excitement of current thinking and controversy. For the teacher and student, the separate self-contained books provide a flexible up-to-date survey of current thinking on each subarea covered and at the same time permit maximum flexibility in course and curriculum design.

EZRA SOLOMON

Contents

Preface

As more and more corporations become involved in international business, their managers are discovering that their corporate training has not fully prepared them for the added problems they are now encountering. International finance problems have been especially troublesome. What is needed is a more complete approach to the study of corporate finance. However, traditional material fails to adequately cover the international dimensions of corporate finance.

The purpose of this book is to supplement the material available in traditional corporate finance texts in order to provide the reader with a broader knowledge of the financial problems and solutions of a firm operating in the "real world," not just in one country. No attempt will be made to adequately cover those aspects that are common to both domestic and international firms. Since most points in domestically oriented corporate finance books hold true in international finance, they will not be repeated. New material—that relevant to the international dimensions—will simply be added.

Although this book could be used in international finance courses, it is not intended to be a complete text of that field. It contains only those aspects of international finance that pertain directly to corporate finance. This book could be used as a supplement to international finance textbooks, but it is primarily intended to aid those interested in corporate finance.

The order of the topics covered is similar to that found in most corporate finance texts. The student need only look at the table of contents of this book to find the chapter relevant to the topic he is currently studying.

There are several people who have greatly assisted in the completion of this book. The author especially appreciates the efforts of Larry E. Tischer, Barry Taylor, Timothy Logan, Jeffrey M. Gardner, Neil Kugelman, Robert A. Peters, Jr., Vivian Opelt, and Roy Cromer and his staff at The College of Administrative Science of Ohio State University.

David A. Ricks

Part One

AN OVERVIEW

Introduction

If the gross national products (GNPs) of countries were compared to the assets of corporations, and if a list of the 100 largest resulting "financial entities" was compiled, only about twenty-five countries would make the list. Fully three-fourths of the world's economic powers are corporations—most of them operating in many countries. These multinational corporations (MNCs) are major influences in world affairs and control assets that are more extensive than all of the resources of some of the countries in which they operate.

Such corporate wealth has never been easy to manage. As these corporations grew they became increasingly complex. The decision to grow by going overseas—a decision which almost all large corporations have made—only added to the complexity of management problems.

Finance has been one of the areas of greatest added complexity and concern for international managers. It is no longer sufficient for the financial manager to limit his study simply to the domestic aspects of corporate finance. Almost every single topic which can be studied in corporate finance now has international dimensions which are equally important.

Each of these topics will be examined, but some are so important that they influence many of the others. These especially important topics will be introduced first. To be specific, the subjects of "risk" and "taxes" must be understood before one can delve very far into the more standard corporate finance problem areas such as working capital management or even capital budgeting.

Risk

The basic concepts concerning risk and uncertainty remain unchanged when venturing into the international arena. But this does not mean that the nature of the risks and uncertainties are the same. Far from it. For one thing, the set is larger. International business managers face extra risks such as changes in currency values, selective control of activities because the corporation is "foreign," and even expropriation.

Additional Risks

Possible currency value changes (usually accompanied by differing rates of inflation) present the financial manager with a host of problems. A major reduction in the local currency value may mean that the earnings sent to the parent company are not worth very much. This assumes that there still are earnings. Such may not even remain the case because costs for supplies from other countries can increase far more than planned. Foreign debt obligations can also be more difficult to meet.

Selective controls are often discriminatory practices used because of political pressures. Tax examiners may require extra data and may be less tolerant. Extra licenses and red tape may be required. Local laws may be more strictly enforced. Not all MNCs face such discrimination, of course, but the risks always exist and must be acknowledged and considered.

The risk of expropriation is also always present. There are ways to reduce it, but it cannot be eliminated or ignored.[1] The general public has the false impression that expropriation of a United States–owned firm by a foreign government is an act of confiscation. In truth, such outright seizures are extremely rare except in times of war between the two countries. Governments almost always pay for the company expropriated. The only real question is *how much*. It is this risk of being forced to sell at a price that may be below the firm's estimated value that must be considered.

At this point, it is natural to ask, "How does one 'consider' these additional risks?" The assessment of the risks, of course, is mandatory and the significance of each risk will depend upon each individual situation. (More on this will be presented in the chapter on capital

[1] See W. R. Hoskins, "How to Counter Expropriation," *Harvard Business Review*, September-October, 1970, p. 102.

budgeting.) Different firms face different degrees of risk in each country, but they *all* face these additional risks.

Misconceptions

This brings us back to the opening remarks about risk. That is, the basic concepts about risk are the same for domestic and international financial managers. However, the fact that international finance involves additional risks leads to important points.

One of the most basic concepts concerning risk and return is the principle that no higher risks should be accepted without higher expected returns. The risk-return concept remains unchanged in international finance. In fact, it is often used to argue that foreign investments may need to promise a higher return than domestic opportunities before the analyst should recommend the project. These demands for higher returns have led some critics of MNCs to cry foul and charge "profiteering" (or at least "excessive profits") when, in fact, the firm is often simply following apparently sound financial practices by looking at *both* risks and returns. Managers ask, "If our firm is not permitted to earn a higher return on foreign operations, then why should it go there and take the added risks?"

It should be noted, though, that risk and return concepts still apply —all of them. This includes the necessity to examine the total risk picture—not just the risk of a single project or the risks in a single country. It may not be an adequate defense for the management of a MNC to claim merely that its firm faces extra risks so it should get higher returns.

Recent studies now indicate that stock market investors holding an internationally diversified portfolio may do better than those holding a totally domestic one.[2] This is true when the standard deviations from the expected rate of return are not very highly correlated to each other (a situation that seems to exist often, though not all the time). So diversification can help in risk reduction when the correlations are low. It is now believed that this same principle is also true for a "portfolio" of direct investments. By investing in many different economies, it may be possible to have such an internationally diversified "portfolio" that it will provide better results and be even less risky than any of the individual opportunities. In other words, it may be possible to accept high-risk projects and yet be taking little overall risk! Of course this would require economies without high degrees of cor-

[2]For example, see the article by Haim Levy and Marshall Sarnat, "International Diversification of Investment Portfolios," *American Economic Review*, September 1970, pp. 668–75.

relation to each other, but it could mean that the MNC need not always require higher rates of return [especially in less-developed countries (LDCs)] in order to invest in risky projects.

Another common belief is that the MNC must have a higher rate of return than local firms in the host country. Many businessmen say that MNCs must be more profitable than local competition because they face more risks, but risk-return principles make no such demands. Returns must be worth the risks, but the returns need not be higher than those made by others. MNCs that will invest only in countries where they can outperform all other firms in the field are much more vulnerable to outside criticism *and* will loose many good investment opportunities where the returns would justify the risks—even the unique international risks of expropriation, discrimination, or currency changes.

The impact of these additional risks will become much more apparent in the following chapters. It is because of these extra risks, though, that many additional techniques have been developed that are unique to international finance. We will return to these new techniques after considering a second set of important new variables—those related to taxes.

Bibliography

Baker, James, and Thomas Bates, *Financing International Business Operations.* Scranton, Pa.: Intext, Inc., 1971.

Battersby, Mark. "Swapping Risk for Reward." *Financial Executive,* May 1975, pp. 22–25.

Eiteman, David, and Arthur Stonehill, *International Business Finance.* Reading, Mass.: Addison-Wesley Publishing Company, Inc., 1973.

Flowers, Edward. "Future Shocks in Multinational Finance." *Atlanta Economic Review,* March 1976, pp. 4–7.

Hoskins, W. R. "How to Counter Expropriation." *Harvard Business Review,* September-October 1970, pp. 102–12.

Lessard, Donald. "World, Country and Industry Relationships in Equity Returns: Implications for Risk Reduction through International Diversification." *Financial Analysts Journal,* January-February 1976, pp. 32–38.

Levy, Haim, and Marshall Sarnat, "International Diversification of Investment Portfolios." *American Economic Review,* September 1970, pp. 668–75.

Nehrt, Lee. *International Finance for Multinational Business,* 2nd ed., Scranton, Pa.: Intext, Inc., 1972.

Pohl, Hermann. "The Coming Era of the Financial Executive." *Business Horizons,* June 1973, pp. 15–22.

Ricks, David A. "An Annotated Bibliography for International Finance." *Journal of Financial Education,* Fall 1973, pp. 92–108.

Rodriguez, Rita, and Eugene Carter, *International Financial Management.* Englewood Cliffs, N.J.: Prentice-Hall, Inc., 1976.

Smith, Don. "Financial Variables in International Business." *Harvard Business Review,* January-February 1966, pp. 93–104.

Solnik, Bruno. "The International Pricing of Risk: An Empirical Investigation of the World Capital Market Structures." *Journal of Finance,* May 1974b, pp. 365–78.

———. "Why Not Diversify Internationally." *Financial Analysts Journal,* July-August 1974, p. 48.

Van Agtmael, Antoine. "How Business has Dealt with Political Risk." *Financial Executive,* January 1976, pp. 26–30.

Wallingford, Buckner A. H., II. "Discussion: The International Pricing of Risk." *Journal of Finance,* May 1974, pp. 392–95.

Weston, J. Fred, and Bart Sorge, *International Managerial Finance.* Homewood, Ill.: Richard D. Irwin, Inc., 1972.

Zenoff, David, and Jack Zwick, *International Financial Management.* Englewood Cliffs, N.J.: Prentice-Hall, Inc., 1969.

Taxes

Certainly one of the most important variables to consider in any type of international business endeavor involves the area of taxation. It is imperative that the potential investor be aware of the different tax systems, concepts, and rates involved before making a final decision as to the profitability and acceptability of any foreign project or investment.

All else being equal, the firm definitely should go to the country where its total tax burden is minimized. Unfortunately, it is very difficult to determine the true tax burden. Tax policies differ from country to country, especially with respect to which income is taxable, acceptable depreciation policies, and taxation of capital gains. Tax treaties between countries must also be considered. Furthermore, different types of international enterprises are taxed differently. There are great differences in the taxation of a foreign branch of a corporation and a subsidiary.

Many of these added complexities are due to the fact that governments have not been able to come to any general agreement on tax policies. Each country has its own claims, concepts, and tax incentives. It is up to the businessman to sort them out and optimize the situation. In order for him to do so, he must have a general understanding of the typical claims, concepts, and incentives.

Global or Territorial Claims

A country has the option of considering all firms in its country as "subjects" of the state and all earnings—regardless of origin—as subject to its taxes. In other words, a country may tax a firm and all its foreign subsidiaries. It need not matter if the foreign income was from investment or services. Such an outlook on tax liability is called "global."

A country may also choose to tax only that income earned within its territory. This "territorial" claim is, of course, much more popular with MNCs, but not as popular with governments. Several financial centers (including Switzerland and Hong Kong) and many Latin American countries do not tax their firms' foreign earnings. Many other countries however, including the United States, believe that their firms must be liable for earnings anywhere in the world.

The global claim creates the probability of double taxation in that the foreign earnings are generally subject to both local and home-country taxes. To reduce this double burden, many countries provide some form of tax credit for taxes paid to foreign governments. Nevertheless, most MNCs feel that the requirement to pay additional taxes to their home country puts them at a competitive disadvantage. Local firms only pay local taxes and, without any second-country tax, can retain and reinvest more and may be able to sell at lower prices and still have a higher after-tax return on investment. This apparently unfair situation may be profitable to governments but runs counter to some tax concepts.

Concepts

Neutrality and Equity

Two of the most basic tax concepts are that taxes should be equitable and neutral. That is to say, taxes should be fair and they should not influence decisions in the economic system. The commonly accepted reasoning for a neutral tax system is that the most *efficient* system is one in which supply and demand are left alone to determine prices and economic actions. However, few people seem to truly want such a system for all situations. Most argue that efficiency isn't everything so governments must set other goals and must sometimes provide tax incentives to attain those goals. Therefore, tax law sometimes provides incentives that no longer resemble an economically neutral system. And when the system is no longer neutral, it often provides opportunities for some and disadvantages to others.

Some form of equity and neutrality is often hoped for, though. It may take the form of taxing all earnings—regardless of origin—at one rate. This global outlook is trying to achieve "domestic neutrality."

Locally (in theory) everyone is treated equally. But unless all countries have the same tax rate, the problem is that MNCs of one country will pay higher taxes than MNCs in other countries and, therefore, will be at a competitive disadvantage abroad.

A second approach is to tax foreign income only enough to make the overall rate of taxation equal to that paid by others in the country from which it is derived. This system is called "foreign neutrality," but it would permit MNCs based in high-tax countries (such as the United States) to retain a larger proportion of before-tax earnings than their domestic counterparts. This, it is argued, would put them at a competitive advantage over domestic firms in the home country and is, therefore, not an equitable policy either.

Dividend Treatment

Even though tax systems do not result in equal treatment for everyone, that is not the biggest problem for MNCs. In fact, a much greater concern is the wide variety of complex systems which must be carefully considered and understood. Take, for example, the various tax treatments of profits. In general, there are three major classes of systems:

1. Single tax. Income is taxed only once. If it is taxed at the corporate level, then no taxes are paid on dividends. If the corporation pays no taxes, then the dividend payments to individuals are treated as regular income.
2. Double taxation. Both the corporation and the recipients of dividends pay taxes on earnings.
3. Partial, double taxation. Special tax considerations are sometimes made to give some relief to dividend recipients. Dividends are generally taxed at a lower rate than other forms of personal income *or* (as is more often the case) distributed corporate earnings are taxed at a lower rate than retained earnings.

Each system must be clearly understood by the MNC in order to best determine dividend and retained earnings policies. Clearly, some subsidiaries should be encouraged, for tax reasons alone, to pay their parent firm a greater percentage of earnings than others. Any MNC that tries to have every subsidiary follow the same remittance policy may be losing opportunities to reduce the total tax burden. It may be sensible for a large domestic conglomerate to standardize financial practices within its country, but this is not good policy for the MNC. Different environments do not easily permit such standardizations.[1]

A great deal more on the treatment and handling of dividends is included in chapter 13.

---

[1]For over a hundred examples of what happens when a MNC fails to consider the foreign environment, see David Ricks, Marilyn Fu, and Jeffrey Arpan, *International Business Blunders* (Columbus, Ohio: Grid, Inc., 1974).

Value Added

One of the more frequently encountered tax concepts (especially used in Western Europe) is known as a "value-added" tax. The idea is to tax all items at each stage of development. Each improvement results in a tax liability, but only for the increased value.

The uniqueness of this concept is that there is no emphasis on profits. In fact, even firms losing money must pay for any product improvement. This causes many problems for poorly managed firms, but rewards efficient ones. It also has the advantage of being rather easy to understand (especially because firms are not permitted to use the many loopholes and special tax laws which are so typical of other tax systems).

Special Incentives

Taxes are more complex internationally, but that does not mean that things are necessarily worse or that all taxes are bad—in fact, the results may be an improvement. Special tax incentives can easily make it worthwhile for the MNC to sort out the various national claims, concepts, and plans.

Government Concessions

Many concessions and incentives are offered by governments in order to attract foreign investment. A common tax incentive is to promise no taxes at all for the first few years (the length of time is often subject to negotiation).

Other countries promise reduced tax rates for new firms. The reduction can be in absolute percentages or by making temporary changes in the normal accounting system. For example, assets may be depreciated at an abnormally high rate.

Still other countries promise tax credits on such things as new investments. The result is a reduction in reported net income subject to the normal tax rate.

Tax Havens

There are a few countries which promise never to tax income—foreign or domestic. Such countries are known as tax havens and have caused a great deal of interest and concern (interest from firms, concern from other governments).

The problem is that such countries provide big temptations for firms to report artificial results by setting false prices during "transfer pricing."

Transfer Pricing

Transfer pricing is the pricing of goods (or services) sold between divisions or subsidiaries of an organization. Even though the goods are still controlled by the parent company, possession and legal ownership are transferred from one part of the organization to another by selling the goods at some agreed upon price. Domestic business sales terms are normally agreed upon with each party considering its own vested interests. This is known as an "arm's-length" approach. Both parties in an arms-length agreement want to obtain the best possible sales terms. But when both parties are owned by one firm, there is an ability to set the price artificially high or low and still complete the sale.

This possibility is sometimes tempting in international operations because it is then possible to reduce total tax payments. The subsidiaries in high-tax countries simply buy materials from the subsidiaries in low-tax countries at high prices and then sell their finished products at low prices to the subsidiaries in the low-tax countries. For example, subsidiary *A* is in a high-tax country while subsidiaries *B* and *C* are in low-tax countries. The parent firm can direct subsidiary *A* to buy supplies from subsidiary *B* at high prices and sell the finished goods to subsidiary *C* at low prices. Both subsidiaries *B* and *C* make extra profits which are not taxed heavily while subsidiary *A* may not make much money at all and, therefore pays very little tax—even though the rate is high. The overall effect is that profits occur in places where they are not heavily taxed so the MNC is able to keep a much greater proportion of its before-tax global earnings.

The only trouble is that governments in high-tax countries don't like this system. They want all transactions to be at prices that would exist if business were done at arm's length. Artificial pricing to the contrary is likely to create problems with the host governments if detected. The temptation to show profits in tax havens is high, but heavy usage of tax havens may not be worth the ill will of other governments.

Of course, the firm also risks more than simply the loss of good will with host governments. If a government concludes that the MNC is trying to avoid taxes, then special fines (or worse) may be imposed. In fact, a few firms have been forced to sell their subsidiaries—at reduced rates—to pay back taxes claimed due because of tax avoidance via transfer pricing.

Furthermore, researchers have concluded that heavy usage of transfer pricing for tax purposes can cause morale problems among employees in high-tax countries.[2] (The firms look less profitable than they are and management fears that they will be undervalued.)

For all of these reasons, it is generally advised that MNCs price goods at arm's length. Firms that have been selling at artificial prices are urged to reconsider the practice before it is detected. Of course, such firms cannot quickly change prices to true rates without creating attention so they are urged to slowly change prices to bring them more into line.

Specific Tax Law

This chapter has introduced the general concepts and conditions which exist in international taxation. A wide variety of governmental claims and outlooks exist and within each one is an entirely unique set of tax laws. Unfortunately, the specifics of tax law for each country are often very complex also. Nevertheless, profit opportunities abroad are great and many firms have also received special tax incentives and concessions from host governments. For many MNCs the effort to sort out tax laws has been worthwhile. However, these firms have not done so without seeking competent international tax lawyers and tax experts in the countries where they have considered doing or presently do business. It is not usually necessary to put such men on permanent employment rolls, but it is essential to at least seek their counsel from time to time. Tax law is too important and too specialized to handle otherwise.

[2]See James Shulman, "When the Price is Wrong by Design," *Columbia Journal of World Business*, May-June 1967, pp. 69–77.

Bibliography

Bartoli, Edward B. "United States Taxation of International Business." *Business Topics*, Summer 1964, pp. 55–62.

Beardwood, Roger. "Sophistication Comes to the Tax Havens." *Fortune*, February 1969, pp. 95–178.

Dreier, Ronald. "U.S. Income Tax Treaties" *Columbia Journal of World Business*, Summer 1975, pp. 21–28.

Eiteman, David, and Arthur Stonehill, *Multinational Business Finance*. Reading, Mass.: Addison-Wesley Publishing Company, Inc., 1973. Pp. 145–87.

Gaskins, Peter. "Taxation of Foreign Source Income." *Financial Analysts Journal*, September-October 1973, pp. 55–64.

Harriss, C. Lowell. "Value-Added Taxation." *Columbia Journal of World Business*, July-August 1971, pp. 78–86.

Howard, Fred. "Overview of International Taxation." *Columbia Journal of World Business*, Summer 1975, pp. 5–11.

Information Guide for U.S. Corporations Doing Business Abroad. New York, N.Y.: Price Waterhouse & Co., January 1972.

Jenks, Thomas. "Taxation of Foreign Income." *George Washington Law Review*, 42 (1974): 537–56.

Kalish, Richard H. "Tax Considerations in Organizing for Business Abroad." *Taxes*, February 1966, pp. 71–86.

Lindholm, Richard W. "Toward a New Philosophy of Taxation." *The Morgan Guaranty Survey*, January 1972, pp. 3–8.

Musgrave, Peggy B. *United States Taxation of Foreign Investment Income*. Cambridge, Mass.: International Tax Program, Harvard Law School, 1969.

Nehrt, Lee. *International Finance for Multinational Business*, 2nd ed. Scranton, Pa.: Intext, Inc., 1972. pp. 591–658.

Ness, Walter. "U.S. Corporate Income Taxation and the Dividend Remittance Policy of MNC's." *Journal of International Business Studies*, Spring 1975, pp. 67–77.

Radler, Albert. "International Capital Markets and Taxation." *Management International Review*, no. 6, 1973, pp. 65–74.

Rodriguez, Rita, and E. Eugene Carter, *International Financial Management*. Englewood Cliffs, N.J.: Prentice-Hall, Inc., 1976. pp. 581–92.

Scott, Robert T. "Tax and Other Implications of the Foreign Direct Investment Regulations." *Taxes*, January 1969, pp. 32–44.

Sherfy, Raphael. "Recent Changes and New Considerations in the International Tax Area." *Taxes*, December 1975, pp. 857–71.

Shulman, James. "When the Price is Wrong by Design." *Columbia Journal of World Business*, May-June 1967, pp. 69–77.

Smith, Dan Throop. "Value-Added Tax: The Case For." *Harvard Business Review*, November-December 1970, pp. 857–71.

Stone, Lawrence. "United States Tax Policy Toward Foreign Earnings of Multinational Corporations." *George Washington Law Review*, 42 (1974): 557–67.

Surrey, Stanley S. "Value-Added Tax: The Case Against." *Harvard Business Review, November-December* 1970, pp. 86–94.

Part Two

WORKING CAPITAL MANAGEMENT

FOR a firm operating within a single country, working capital management involves the use of certain prescribed aids such as cost forecasting, inventory models, credit standards, and financing procedures. Operations that are conducted abroad, however, must take into account several additional features associated with an increased degree of financial risk. Chief among the added risks is the potential loss from foreign exchange inflation or devaluation. In part 2 we will describe those unique procedures which, when followed by a firm overseas, will improve the management of its working capital accounts facing the added risks of complex international conditions.

Analysis of the broad category of working capital necessitates a study of each account within that group. In taking a broad overview, however, one should initially note some of the operating characteristics associated with a financially uncertain environment so as to more easily develop various precautionary measures. One of the biggest problems facing MNCs is that subsidiaries operate under various rates of inflation. Among the adverse effects of inflationary business conditions are (1) difficulty in obtaining credit and high cost of credit, (2) buildup of accounts receivable and lengthening of collection periods, (3) governmental imposition of price controls, (4) lack of available funds for replacement of assets, (5) decrease in competitive advantage of goods which are exported from an inflationary country, and (6) increasing labor costs as inflation erodes workers' purchasing power. To combat these problems, a firm must concentrate on (1) defending its profit-earning ability and (2) maintaining the real value of its assets.

There are many ways to do this. For one thing, it is generally beneficial for a company to reduce working capital accounts that originate in countries with high rates of inflation. A second strategy is to build up accounts receivable which originate in countries having little inflation and strong currencies. These and other practices will be discussed in the following three chapters which cover three major areas of working capital management: cash management, accounts receivable management, and inventory management.

3

Cash Management

THE general principles that apply to cash management on an international basis are often very similar to those used by many firms domestically. The overall cash management objective for any corporation is to control its liquid assets with the goal of optimizing corporate fund utilization. However, the parameters within which the MNC operates are much broader, much more complex, and their interrelationships are constantly changing. Obvious, but important, considerations are the distances and the cultural differences between organizational units which complicate the process of information flows, forecasting, and control.

Another difference between domestic and international cash management is the increase internationally in possible sources and uses of funds. This added variety and complexity is illustrated in Figure 3-1. It should be noted that MNCs do not usually need to be in a country to consider using that country's money and capital markets. Therefore, in reality, most countries of the world can and should be considered in cash management policy making and implementation.

Obviously, the need to consider such a large number of financial markets adds a host of new variables. These include tax concepts, governmental restrictions on such things as intracompany funds flows and the repatriations of profits, and differences in cultures. For example, cash balances in Western Europe are generally higher than in the

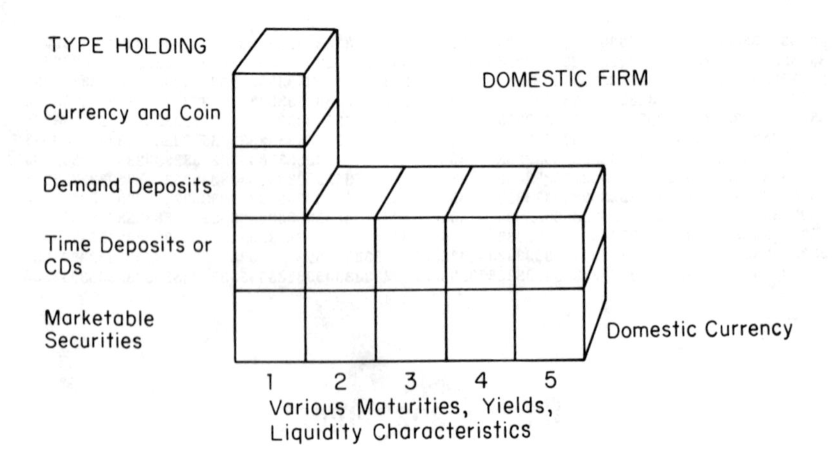

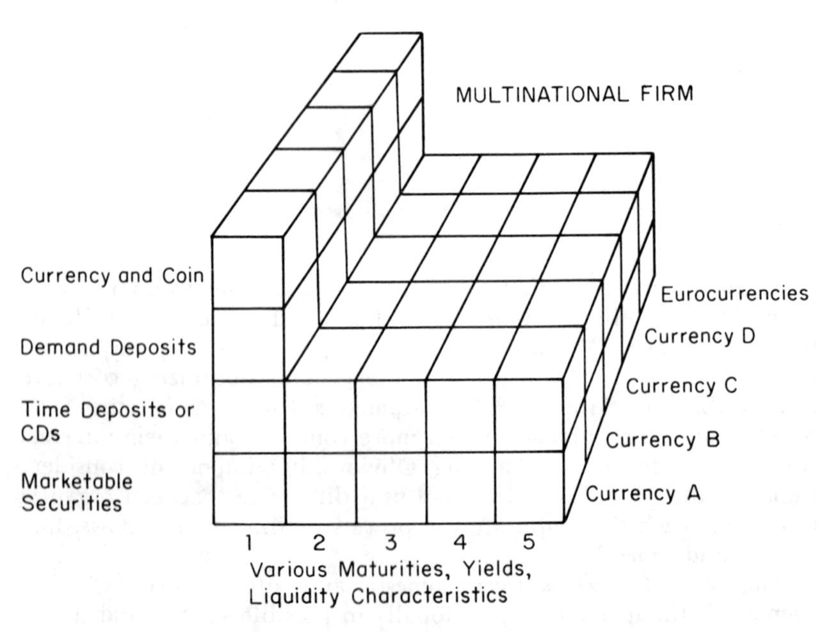

Figure 3-1. Liquid Asset Possibilities

SOURCES David K. Eiteman and Arthur I. Stonehill, *Multinational Business Finance* (Reading, Mass.: Addison-Wesley Publishing Company, Inc., 1973), p. 293.

United States because more transactions are conducted in cash. These differences must be incorporated into the management system.

In general, managers try to keep cash balances to a minimum in order to invest in profit-making ventures. And just like firms in the United States, MNCs want to speed up the collections and deposit of cash. In the United States, speed is often achieved by having many banks so that deposits are made locally. Versions of this are also possible overseas—but sometimes with important differences. In some countries, for instance, there is no such thing as a checking account and payments are often made in cash—at local post offices. Naturally, the MNC must adjust its systems and establish accounts at the post offices.

The problem of float, funds immobilized during the fund transfer process, also differs between domestic and international transactions. Float from a domestic point of view involves only the temporary loss of income of these funds. In international operations, however, the problem is twofold. It involves the loss of income on the funds tied up during the longer transfer process as well as their exposure to foreign exchange-rate risk during the transfer period. Naturally, the MNC wants to cut down the float time as much as possible.

As the multinational firm attempts to conduct business on an effective and efficient commercial basis across national boundaries, it is likely to be affected by conflicts between the political and economic policies of the several nations involved. Under these policies, governments attempt to achieve their national goals by requiring both domestic and international funds to be used. For this reason, multinational firms have to obey an endless stream of objectives aimed at maximizing the foreign exchange reserves of the host country. For example, the movement of large sums of money is often possible domestically, but it is not as tolerated overseas. Movement of funds across international boundaries is often not permitted since it will cause pressures on a country's currency exchange rate. Such governmental restrictions prevent the multinational firms from carrying out optimal cash management. The MNC must be satisfied with operations performed in a complex set of environments which contain a host of suboptimizing constraints.

The Flow of Funds

In order to carry out its operations, the multinational firm causes a steady flow of funds to take place between parent and subsidiaries and branches as well as among the subsidaries and branches themselves. These flows are rather unique and will be looked at one at a time.

Subsidiary to Parent Fund Flow

The principal flow of funds here is for goods received from the parent and to pay dividends, interest on loans, principal reduction payments, royalty payments, license fees, technical service fees, management fees, and export commissions.

It should be noted that the parent does not have total control in the magnitude of the flow of funds. A chronic foreign exchange shortage in a country is likely to force severe restrictions on the amount of dividend payments. Additionally, many governments impose a dividend withholding tax at the time dividends are remitted to foreign owners. A further complexity exists in the case of joint ventures. Local partners often object to large dividend payments to the parent company because they view this as a danger to the liquidity of the venture. (They are, after all, usually not as worried about currency risks of their own currency—more will be said about this at the end of the chapter.)

Interest on loans is usually permitted to be paid and is fully taxable to the recipient in most countries, but is also fully deductible from the subsidiary's income.

There are more restrictions on returning loan principal than on paying interest, but the restrictions are usually known in advance and such payments are seldom totally forbidden.

Royalty and licensing fees in general are regarded as valid obligations to foreign firms; however, they may be limited to a particular percentage of sales.

Technical service and management fees must reflect service actually rendered. Otherwise, a government taxing authority will levy additional taxes or penalties.

Parent to Subsidiary Fund Flow

The largest flow of funds here is usually the initial investment. Often, however, the subsidiary will receive additional funds in the form of loans or added investments.

Subsidiary to Subsidiary Fund Flow

Subsidiaries may loan funds to each other or purchase goods from each other. When done on a large scale, this provides an opportunity to regulate the flow of funds to and from any particular subsidiary. Funds from one subsidiary may also be used to invest in the creation of another. When such investments are made, it is often the choice of home management that all dividend and principal repayments go directly to the home office. This need not be the case, however, and it is possible for subsidiaries to have cash flows similar to parent company flows.

All these intracompany flows will be much more fully discussed in chapter 10.

Foreign Exchange Problems

As has been previously explained, businessmen who operate in the international arena are faced with many problems which domestic businessmen are able to avoid or ignore. However, the various cash flow patterns just discussed are not the biggest problem. In fact, of all the additional problems, those generated by currency differences and exchange-rate risks have been the most frequently encountered.[1] In a review of 109 currencies between 1948 and 1967, for example, 1 currency appreciated in value and all but 12 of the others declined in value (21 were devalued at least three times and 62 devaluations were each for more than forty percent).[2] No wonder MNCs encounter currency problems so frequently!

With the problem of devaluation so widespread, it is important for the MNC to have some rational system for handling it. The threat of a devaluation often disrupts the normal operating procedure of subsidiaries in the threatened country. Capital expenditures are often postponed or local currency borrowing may be increased in an effort to offset exposed assets and reduce net exposure. Capital remittances to the parent may be speeded through dividends, royalties, transfer pricing changes, or a variety of fees, as well as repayment of debt or interest payments. The local subsidiary must be able to finance these drains or operate on the remaining funds. The subsidiary should not hold excess cash under these conditions and funds should be reallocated to other areas of the world system, but these techniques are effective and feasible only to the extent that government regulations permit, local financing is available, and the added costs of transfers are less than the expected losses from devaluation. Thus it is required that the manager have accurate forecasts not only of the probability of devaluations, but also of their probable amount. In order to attempt such esitmates, the forecaster must know what causes currency values to change.

---

[1]Raymond Vernon, *Manager in the International Economy* (Englewood Cliffs, N.J.: Prentice-Hall, Inc., 1968), p. 3.

[2]Bernard Lietaer, *Financial Management of Foreign Exchange* (Cambridge, Mass.: M.I.T. Press, 1971), pp. 1–6.

ors which affect exchange rates include:

iflations
ty
ons
4. ... e and balance of payments changes
5. Changes ... a country's international monetary reserves (gold, foreign exchange, and International Monetary Fund position)
6. Psychological pressures against currencies (speculation)
7. Monetary and fiscal policy
8. Ties to other currencies
9. Interest rates

Many of these factors are highly subjective and difficult to quantify. Even if the firm has accurately analyzed the economic pressures against a currency, the influence of governmental policy may alter the rate of change so it is often quite difficult to be sure what will happen, when it will happen, and, therefore, how to best protect the firm.

Protection

A firm's susceptibility to exchange losses is usually measured in terms of net exposure defined as exposed assets minus exposed liabilities. This represents the monetary value that would be affected by a currency devaluation. It is relevant only for firms with transactions or accounts denominated in foreign currencies. Transactions exposure is the risk that results when sales or purchases are denominated in a foreign currency, while translation exposure is the risk of changes in the valuation of balance sheet accounts denominated in other currencies that are valued at current rather than historical exchange rates.

There are many ways to reduce a firm's net exposure. As a general rule, a firm would like to maintain its asset accounts in hard currencies and denominate its liability accounts in soft currencies. Other procedures available to protect exposed items include:

1. Speeding payments of profits from weak currency subsidiaries to the parent through profit remittance channels
2. Delaying investments in weak currency subsidiaries
3. Increasing local liabilities in weak currency subsidiaries
4. Speeding payments denominated in hard currencies

5. Self-insuring through reserves (putting some earnings into a special account in order to cover exchange losses)
6. Arranging protection in the forward exchange market (obtaining guarantees to sell or buy a currency at a predetermined price and time)
7. Currency swapping (covering a weak currency being obtained by buying a forward contract to sell it later)[3]

The decisions about protection strategies are largely dependent on the attitude of management toward risk. The risk can be spread over time in small amounts or the risk of loss in a single period can be borne by seeking no protection. Since American firms generally favor steady increases in earnings per share (EPS) in terms of United States currency, they tend to avoid the risk of large losses in a single period and seek protection, often in the forward exchange market, so that the short-term costs are a small percentage of overall potential losses.

In evaluating the alternative protective instruments, the manager must examine several cost factors. The opportunity cost of alternative investments is difficult to measure but is important. Another relevant cost is that of transferring funds which includes clerical costs and management time spent instituting the transfer. The effective borrowing cost is an obvious consideration and the cost of possible exchange-rate losses has already been mentioned.

Of course the best time to buy a forward contract or to use any other method of protection is hard to determine. All economic factors may be correctly identified and analyzed, but unpredictable political factors can profoundly influence currency rate changes (or at least the rate of these changes). The timing of protection is, therefore, very difficult. Protection against exposed accounts should be sought before major currency declines. However, as devaluation grows more likely, the costs of protection increase at an increasing rate (if the options even remain). The challenge is to obtain protection when the expected value is highest.

In order to do this, some estimate of devaluation probabilities is necessary. But accurate estimates are hard to derive and require an accurate reporting system. The day-to-day working capital decisions of subsidiaries are often decentralized; cash needs are forecast locally and banking is handled locally. However, in order to increase the efficiency of risk management and information flows, centralized cash-mobilization centers are becoming increasingly prevalent. Many companies have found that a centralized depository allows many econ-

---

[3]Many versions of this exist. Besides currency swaps, there are credit swaps, covered interest arbitrage, and "arbi" loans. A description of all these forward exchange contract options goes beyond the scope of this book but such data are readily available in any international finance textbook. See also pp. 80–81 of this book.

omies of scale, specialization, and better worldwide perspectives on risks and investment opportunities for excess cash.

When a centralized depository is used, subsidiaries are encouraged to hold minimum transactions balances and no precautionary reserves in order to reduce risks. Excess cash is transferred by wire or telex to the central fund for reallocation, thus freeing larger sums of cash and reducing the amount of funds needed for worldwide protection. These centers are generally established in countries with well-developed capital and foreign exchange markets, stable governments and currencies, liberal tax regulations, and minimal restrictions on the flow of funds. The process allows for better control, profitability, and efficiency in managing and evaluating the subjective variables which influence the amount of exchange rate risk for the firm.

Models

Some of the many factors which must be examined by the central office in determining optimal cash levels in different countries are the following:

1. Rates of return earned on excess funds
2. Liquidity and risk factors
3. Transfer costs
4. Devaluation pressures
5. Advantages of cash funds in bank accounts for later loan requests
6. Governmental restrictions on funds transfers
7. Short-term investment opportunities

With so many variables, it should come as no surprise to discover that more and more managers are looking for computer models which can keep track of the situation, "analyze" it, make forecasts, and then make recommendations. Various methods have been attempted, mostly in the form of theoretical models.

David Rutenberg was one of the first to develop a model for liquid asset management.[4] His rather complex, theoretical model was developed about the same time as the model by Robert Shulman.[5] Shulman's model was intended to determine when the exposure risk dictated coverage in the forward market.

Bernard Lietaer probably received the most attention when he in-

[4]David Rutenberg, "Maneuvering Liquid Assets in a Multinational Company: Formulation of Deterministic Solution Procedures," *Management Science,* June 1970, pp. B671–84.

[5]Robert Shulman, "Are Foreign Exchange Risks Measurable?" *Columbia Journal of World Business,* May-June 1970, pp. 55–60.

troduced his model that same year.[6] Lietaer's model was especially interesting because he first explained the problem and presented the complexities with a set of unique diagrams.[7]

Unfortunately, these models required probability estimates of the size and time of devaluations. The assumptions were made that they were available, but this author (and many others) has tried to develop accurate forecasting techniques with only limited results.[8] Without correct forecasts, the models are interesting and useful in theory, but are not immediately useful in the business world.

A subsequent model by Alan Shapiro and David Rutenberg limited the problem to an examination of costs.[9] Noting that protection costs the firm in one form or another, their model concentrated on determining those costs and estimating the appropriate time to incur them. However, their model also assumed forecasting ability.

Several other models have also been developed. W. Randolf Folks took a control-theory approach and developed a multiperiod model using various expected utility criteria.[10] De Faro and Jucker looked at borrowing under various conditions[11] and Naumann-Etienne used linear programming to find optimal cash sources under conditions of certainty.[12]

The assumptions and limitations of these models have tended to to discourage their widespread usage in the business world. If foreign exchange risks can be easily and efficiently eliminated, no one is talking about it. In fact, a growing number of researchers in the field now suspect that the international money and capital markets may be almost as efficient as the United States markets. Trends in exchange rates admittedly exist, but there may be no way to take advantage of

---

[6]Bernard Lietaer, "Managing Risks in Foreign Exchange," *Harvard Business Review*, March-April 1970, pp. 127–38.

[7]A complete presentation of his model subsequently was published in his book, *Financial Management of Foreign Exchange: An Optional Technique to Reduce Risk* (Cambridge, Mass.: M.I.T. Press, 1971).

[8]Perhaps the best work on this problem has been by Martin Murenbeeld, "Economic Factors for Forecasting Foreign Exchange Rate Changes," *Columbia Journal of World Business*, Summer 1975, pp. 81–95. He explains a system for determining probabilities of devaluations, but cannot forecast the size of the change.

[9]Alan Shapiro and David Rutenberg, "When to Hedge Against Devaluation," *Management Science*, August 1974, pp. 1514–30.

[10]W. R. Folks, "The Optimal Level of Forward Transactions," *Journal of Financial and Quantitative Analysis*, January 1973, pp. 105–10. Also see his article, "Decision Analysis for Exchange Risk Management," *Financial Management*, Winter 1972, pp. 101–2.

[11]Clovis de Faro and James Jucker, "The Impact of Inflation and Devaluation on the Selection of an International Borrowing Source," *Journal of International Business Studies*, Fall 1973, pp. 97–104.

[12]R. Naumann-Etinne, "A Framework for Financial Decisions in MNC's—Summary of Recent Research," in *Proceedings of the Tenth Annual Meetings of the Western Finance Associations*, June 9–11, 1974, pp. 859–74.

them in the foreign exchange market without paying for the full value —unless you have inside information.[13]

Summary

The basic techniques and principles of cash management are often the same for both domestic and international corporations. The processes of limiting idle funds and investing excess cash as profitably as possible at the lowest total cost hold in both cases. The differences stem primarily from the fact that there are more variables and more risks involved in international cash management. The larger variety of sources and uses of funds can often be handled by domestic cash management models. These models are especially effective in incorporating added governmental or policy constraints. However, the effect of possible exchange losses resulting from operations in currencies other than that of the parent is a problem not adequately handled by current domestic models. Thus the majority of literature in international cash management deals with models to handle the added dimension of currency risk. Different tax policies, varying governmental policies toward transfer of funds and remittance of profits, and foreign investment alternatives have generally proven amenable to classical manipulation.

As in the domestic case, a majority of the multinational models require very accurate reporting systems and forecasting techniques for the quantification of subjective factors. The most effective and operational models in both cases seem to be the programming models which allow sensitivity analyses to determine probable changes in costs and returns as a result of changes in input variables.

No single model has yet been developed to fully cover all aspects of exchange-rate risks, but the models described above have gone a long way towards examining the problems, interrelationships, and techniques necessary for risk reduction and protection.

---

[13]An excellent article on this subject is Ian Giddy and Gunter Dufey's "The Random Behavior of the Flexible Exchange Rates: Implications for Forecasting," *Journal of International Business Studies*, Spring 1975, pp. 1–32.

Bibliography

Ankrom, Robert. "Top Level Approach to the Foreign Exchange Problem." *Harvard Business Review,* July 1974, pp. 79–90.

Bradford, S. R. "Measuring the Cost of Forward Exchange Contracts." *Euromoney,* August 1974, pp. 71–75.

Denis, Jack, Jr. "How Well Does the International Monetary Market Track the Interbank Forward Market?" *Financial Analysts Journal,* January-February 1976, pp. 50–54.

Eiteman, David, and Arthur Stonehill, *Multinational Business Finance.* Reading, Mass.: Addison-Wesley Publishing Company, Inc., 1973. pp. 289–315.

Falcon, William. *Financing International Operations.* New York, N.Y.: American Management Association, 1965.

Folks, W. R. "Decision Analysis for Exchange Risk Management." *Financial Management,* Winter 1972, pp. 101–2.

———. "The Optimal Level of Forward Transactions." *Journal of Financial and Quantitative Analysis,* January 1973, pp. 105–10.

———, and Stanley Stansell, "The Use of Discriminant Analysis in Forecasting Exchange Rate Movements." *Journal of International Business Studies,* Spring 1975, pp. 33–50.

Giddy, Ian, and Gunter Dufey, "The Random Behavior of the Flexible Exchange Rates: Implications for Forecasting." *Journal of International Business Studies,* Spring 1975, pp. 1–32.

Goeltz, Richard. "Economic Factors in Forecasting Currency Changes." *Columbia Journal of World Business,* January 1973, pp. 73–77.

Gray, Alan K. "Foreign Exchange Forecasting—How Far Can the Computer Help?" *Euromoney*, July 1974, pp. 36–43.

Gull, Don. "Composite Foreign Exchange Risk." *Columbia Journal of World Business*, May 1975, pp. 51–69.

Hackett, John. "New Financial Strategies for the MNC." *Business Horizons*, April 1975, pp. 13–20.

Heckerman, Donald. "The Exchange Risk of Foreign Operations." *Journal of Business*, January 1972, pp. 42–48.

Lietaer, Bernard. *Financial Management of Foreign Exchange*. Cambridge, Mass.: M.I.T. Press, 1971.

———. "Managing Risks in Foreign Exchange." *Harvard Business Review*, March-April 1970, pp. 127–38.

Makin, John. "The Portfolio Method of Managing Foreign Exchange Risk." *Euromoney*, August 1976, pp. 58–64.

Mehta, Dileep, and Iski Inselbag, "Working Capital Management of a Multinational Firm." In *Multinational Business Operations—Financial Management*, edited by S. Sethi and J. Sheth, pp. 56–79. Pacific Palisades, Calif.: Goodyear, 1973.

Meister, Irene. *Managing the International Financial Function*. New York: The National Industrial Conference Board, 1970.

Murenbeeld, Martin. "Economic Factors for Forecasting Foreign Exchange Rate Changes." *Columbia Journal of World Business*, Summer 1975, pp. 81–95.

Naumann-Etinne, R. "A Framework for Financial Decisions in MNC's—Summary of Recent Research." In *Proceedings of the Tenth Annual Meetings of the Western Finance Association*, June 1974, pp. 859–74.

Porter, Frederick. "Forecasting Exchange Rates." *Euromoney*, September 1973, pp. 31–33.

Prindl, R. Andreas. "Guidelines for MNC Money Manager." *Harvard Business Review*, January-February 1976, pp. 73–80.

———. "Managing Exchange Exposure in a Floating World." *Euromoney*, March 1974, pp. 23–27.

Proceedings of Working Capital Management in Advanced Technological Societies Conference, Urbana: University of Illinois, April 1975.

Robbins, Sidney, and Robert Stobaugh, *Money in the Multinational Enterprise*. New York: Basic Books, Inc., 1973.

Rodriguez, Rita, and Eugene Carter, *International Financial Management*. Englewood Cliffs, N.J.: Prentice-Hall, Inc., 1976. pp. 95–220.

Rutenberg, David. "Maneuvering Liquid Assets in a Multinational Company: Formulation and Deterministic Solution Procedures." *Management Science*, June 1970, pp. B671–84.

Serfass, William D., Jr. "You Can't Outguess the Foreign Exchange Market." *Harvard Business Review*, March 1976, pp. 134–37.

Shapiro, Alan. "Exchange Rate Changes, Inflation, and the Value of the Multinational Corporation." *Journal of Finance*, May 1975, pp. 485–502.

———, and David Rutenberg, "When to Hedge Against Devaluation." *Management Science*, August 1974, pp. 1514–30.

Shulman, Robert. "Are Foreign Exchange Risks Measurable?" *Columbia Journal of World Business*, May-June 1970, pp. 55–60.

———. "Corporate Treatment of Exchange Risk." *Journal of International Business Studies*, Spring 1970, pp. 83–88.

Teck, Alan. "Control Your Exposure to Foreign Exchange." *Harvard Business Review*, January 1974, pp. 66–75.

Vernon, Raymond, and Louis Wells, *Manager in the International Economy*. 3rd ed., Englewood Cliffs, N.J.: Prentice-Hall, Inc., 1976.

Waterman, Merwin. "Financial Management in Multinational Corporations." *Michigan Business Review*, January 1968, pp. 10–16; and March 1968, pp. 26–32.

Weston, J. Fred, and Bart W. Sorge, *International Managerial Finance*. Homewood, Ill.: Richard D. Irwin, Inc., 1972. pp. 234–47.

Wooster, J. T., and G. R. Thoman, "New Financial Priorities for MNC's," *Harvard Business Review*, May-June 1974, pp. 58.

Wundisch, Karl. "Centralized Cash Management Systems for the Multinational Enterprise." *Management International Review* 13 (no. 6, 1973): 43–57.

Zenoff, David, and Jack Zwick, *International Financial Management*. Englewood Cliffs, N.J.: Prentice-Hall, Inc., 1969. Chapters 3 and 7.

4

Accounts Receivable Management

ACCOUNTS receivable management is the second important field in working capital management that domestic firms and multinational corporations must deal with in different ways. The truly unique problem area that must be understood by the accounts receivable manager of a MNC concerns the risk of currency value changes.

Currency Value Problems

The accounts receivable manager wants to reduce the risks his firm faces. In order to reduce accounts receivable risks, he should take all actions which cost less than their perceived value. There are several ways he may be able to do this. One of the most commonly used techniques during very risky times is to require that any promised payments to the company are to be made in "hard currencies." That is to say, payments are to be made in currencies that are likely to face little or no devaluation on the currency exchange market. This reduces losses that might be incurred if the payment had been promised in a soft currency that was likely to decline in value before actual payment is made.

Many times, because exchange risk probabilities are so hard to calculate accurately, an MNC may avoid accepting accounts receivable in foreign currencies altogether. Such action, however, is very drastic and is seldom warranted. The lost business opportunities make it difficult to justify the decision. The need to deal in foreign currencies, possibly soft, may be great enough that the MNC should take advantage of the situation even though the risks are high. After all, if the price for the goods or service is increased to a high enough level, currency risks can be easily covered. The trick, of course, is to determine the added risks (a task which was discussed in the previous chapter) and then estimate the price elasticity of demand. If the demand is elastic enough to permit profitable business in a risky currency, then there is no reason to refuse business opportunities even though they are not possible in hard currencies.

It is often possible to purchase currency risk insurance. United States exporters, for example, may buy protection from the Foreign Credit Insurance Association (FCIA). Whether the insurance premium is considered a bargain or not depends upon the firm's perception of the risks it faces and its willingness to take those risks. After all, an MNC may "self-insure," so to speak, by deducting sums from current profits to establish or increase accounting reserves available for possible future losses. Although this system does not really lower actual exchange rate losses, it does allow the company to spread its losses over several accounting periods.

With any of these risk adjustment methods, the firm has to recover its added expenses, usually by charging more for its product. But this need not be the case in all instances. The firm may be able to sell the accounts receivable to a local company which does not need to worry about (or, therefore, charge for) currency charge risks of the MNC.[1] Such sales of accounts receivable are made to businesses known as factoring companies.

Factoring

Factoring is a process whereby a firm sells its accounts receivables. In the United States this is usually done on a notification basis—the invoices received by customers notify them to pay the factor. Overseas, however, nonnotification is more common. Nonnotification is used especially by manufacturers and wholesalers who sell to retail stores and thus have many small accounts with seasonal fluctuations. The client then collects his own receivables and keeps his own books, resulting in a lower fee charged to the client.

There are two types of factoring—maturity and old-line (often called "advance"). Maturity factoring appeals to those clients not presently in liquidity straitjackets who want the services provided by the factor—credit checking, bookkeeping, and collecting from custom-

[1]A complete explanation and illustration of this concept is continued in the discussion of leasing in chapter 12.

ers. Clients are paid for receivables on an average due date calculated monthly. This serves as a continuous source of working funds on a flexible basis. There has been a strong and growing trend towards maturity factoring, not only in the United States but especially in Great Britain. Old-line factoring, the more common and better-known type, provides services and pays the client up to ninety percent upon invoicing. Other services provided by the factor include advanced computer facilities (which might not otherwise be available to many smaller firms) and extensive management services, such as total inventory control, invoicing, sales analysis, and salesman commission reports.

The firms taking advantage of factoring in the United States are similar to those who do so in other nations. Some characteristics these firms often have in common are collection problems, liquidity problems, and, in particular, rapid growth. Firms with highly seasonal sales also seek factoring. Typically these industries are textile and apparel (the long-time factor clientele accounting for eighty-five percent of United States factoring volume in 1970), consumer goods, light engineering products, electronic components, and office equipment. Annual sales for most of these firms are $5–15 million.[2]

Many people, particularly some bankers, feel that factoring is strictly an emergency option to be used in times of tight money or before a firm faces economic death situations. This old image of factoring, a shady money lending operation associated with outrageous interest rates, is being dispelled rapidly as competition in many countries has reduced unwarranted practices.

The costs of factoring are twofold. There is the standard service commission which ranges from three-fourths of one percent to two percent. In the case of advanced factoring interest is also charged, usually three percent above the prime rate.

The effects of factoring may be seen in the cash flow: an improved current ratio (providing higher lines of credit), a higher turnover ratio, and higher profits—"in many cases, a fifteen percent increase or more within nine months of factoring."[3] Accompanying this is a recognition and appreciation by some end customers of a more efficient accounts receivables system.

In export and import transactions, there has been a growing tendency to centralize the accounting function in order to provide more efficient systems. Factors assume all credit, currency, and political risks, provide establishment of letters of credit, arrange loans, make advances for import duties and freight, factor the resultant receivables, and discuss problems. There is immediate conversion of value of sales at

[2]David I. Fisher, "Factoring—An Industry on the Move," *Conference Board Record*, April 1972, p. 43.

[3]R. A. Pilcher, "Factoring—A New Banking Service,'" *Banker*, May 1972, p. 678.

the time of export as a credit in the exporter's local currency. Since factoring is done almost exclusively on a relatively low-volume, short-term basis, risk charges are usually minimal. This type of international factoring, therefore, is similar to a banker's letter of credit for which it can often be used as a substitute. This removal of obstacles of payment and rapid transmission of funds obviously helps increase the firm's cash flow.

Some large banks have estabilshed cooperative arrangements with factoring firms in Europe and the Far East. Still others handle only domestic sales in the United States for foreign firms.

American banks have been instrumental in rapidly enlarging the field of international factoring. There used to be two dozen small- and medium-sized factors and a few giants. Since 1963, when the U.S. Comptroller of the Currency ruled factoring a proper area for national bank expansion, there has been a mass entrance by American banks not only domestically, but especially in Great Britain and continuing through Europe and gradually into the rest of the world.

Banks easily fit into the mold of factors with their bookkeeping and credit checking assets (the most cumbersome aspects of factoring) as well as manpower and computer hardware. There is also the profit potential of higher interest rates. It is an additional service that a bank can offer its customers, especially in encouragement of overseas expansion. And because of the nature of factoring, the client sees the factor on a nearly daily basis—making the customer more aware of other bank services and facilities.

Problems

Because banks have done so well in this field, the U.S. Justice Department is becoming increasingly concerned with a potential concentration of economic power. It is feared that the smaller factors, who rely on these same banks for borrowing funds, may not get as much consideration as the banks' own factoring department. Foreign governments and central banks are also looking (with their vested interests) at the American banks' international dominance. These governmental agencies would like to see competition grow, but there is an inherent restriction because of a shortage of trained personnel.

Other major problems concern legal restrictions on international factoring. The United States adopted the Uniform Commercial Code (UCC) after a long history of disorganized and uncoordinated legal actions and decisions. In Europe, though, only Belgium has made a concerted effort towards some uniform legislation in regards to factoring. In some nations factors face extra exchange controls. Governments and central banks are very concerned with sources of funds (although by and large the rule of thumb is to have arrangements with the respective host countries' central banks). A factor, depending on the country's laws, must take the form of a bank (as in Germany, unless the government gives its approval), a financial establishment, or an ordinary corporation (as in Italy). Furthermore, costs often have to be minutely enumerated lest the host government claim that the factor is charging too high an interest rate.

Tied in with the legal problems are the diverse tax structures which often tax profits due to risks taken at a much lower rate than profits due to services provided by factors. The problem, then, is to determine which part of the profits is to pay for risks taken and which part is for services rendered. Since each country seems to have a different method of determining this, a factoring firm needs legal and tax experts.

Conclusions

In conclusion, international factoring has distinct advantages to offer to many firms. It should, therefore, come as no surprise that the number and size of international factoring firms is growing.

Although international factoring has no uniform laws and must take many forms, there is an apparent trend of administrative attitudes and law which is becoming discernible. Current trends appear to be reducing barriers and aiding international factors in providing better services.[4]

---

[4]Samuel Pisar, "Legal Aspects of International Factoring," *Business Lawyer*, July 1970, p. 1510.

Bibliography

Eiteman, David, and Arthur Stonehill, *Multinational Business Finance*. Reading, Mass.: Addison-Wesley Publishing Company, Inc., 1973. pp. 300–303.

Fisher, David I. "Factoring—An Industry on the Move." *Conference Board Record*, April 1972, p. 43.

Pilcher, R. A. "Factoring—A New Banking Service." *Banker*, May 1972, p. 678.

Pisar, Samuel. "Legal Aspects of International Factoring." *Business Lawyer*, July 1970, p. 1510.

5

Inventory Management

THE inventory account is the third area of working capital which should be analyzed from an international perspective. As with cash and accounts receivable, management of the inventory account requires special procedures and policies in order to cope with a financially uncertain environment.

Introduction

In domestic or one-country operations, a company will attempt to balance its inventory level in a manner such that the carrying cost is less than the costs associated with inventory stockouts such as loss of sales and the opportunity costs of idle plant, equipment, and labor. Various models may be used to determine the appropriate inventory level when operating under a certain set of production conditions. Within the international environment, however, differentials in the costs of production and storage enable the international firm to maintain more flexible inventory policies. A multinational firm can take advantage of the cheaper costs that may exist in a particular country at any particular time by shifting its production or storage function to that area. Counter to this advantage of processing and storing selectivity, however, are tariff levels and other forms of import restriction used by governments. A firm must account for these costs, as well, in determining its inventory policies.

Should the situation exist in which economic and political conditions are stable throughout the world, the multinational firm could easily determine its inventory policy under the above conditions through decisions coordinated by the company headquarters. It is well known, however, that factors such as price levels, currency exchange rates, tariff levels, and political attitudes are indeed variable. Furthermore, one country or region of the world may experience changes in economic conditions at a much faster rate than other areas. Under such conditions, a firm must learn to adjust its policies so as to avoid the loss associated with adverse changes in the environment. To aid this adjustment, decentralization of decision making is often required because decisions must often be made by those who interact on a day-to-day basis with local personnel. Inventory policies require coordinated action through a headquarters division that can ascertain the overall economic conditions of its subsidiaries and permit independent actions by individual subsidiaries each taking advantage of its familiarity with local information and contracts.

Problems Due to Inflation

One major concern to multinational companies is the level of inventory that should be maintained for a particular subsidiary. Given the fact that many foreign subsidiaries and branches operate under inflationary economic conditions, it is important that firms consider the effects of an increasing local price level or devaluation when determining inventory quantities. Of importance to this decision is the type of inventory normally stocked by a subsidiary and the price control regulations within a particular country. If imported goods comprise the majority of the inventory account, the value of inventory in dollar figures will remain the same after a devaluation by the local country if the price of those goods in local currency (LC) may be raised to the original dollar equivalent. Countering this favorable condition is the possibility that the local country may impose price control regulations on its products during inflationary conditions or following a devaluation. Should this be the case, the subsidiary would be unable to raise its prices to the original dollar equivalent and a loss on sales would result. Similarly, inventories acquired locally would decrease in dollar value upon devaluation since undercutting by local competitors would discourage the raising of prices. Depending on the type of inventory and the nature of price controls, a company would adjust its inventory levels to minimize the total cost resulting from exchange fluctuations.

After reviewing the effects of inflationary conditions on the inventory account of a firm, one can develop some standard policies for inventory management. For firms that maintain inventories acquired locally or that operate in a country that uses price controls during inflation, it is necessary to minimize the inventory account in order to avoid dollar loss from devaluation. For example, should the local country declare a ten percent devaluation of its currency in relation to the dollar or should the value decline ten percent against the dollar, firms operating in that country would experience a ten percent reduction in dollar value of their inventory since inventories are typically translated at current rather than historical rates. (More will be said later about the various accounting practices used in such situations.) Similarly, a firm that imports its finished or semifinished goods (as do most foreign subsidiaries and branches) would need to minimize the amounts of these goods if price controls are enforced by the local government. Should a devaluation occur, imported goods sold under government-regulated prices would result in a degree of profit reduction for the firm depending on the extent of price restriction. Thus, maintaining low inventory accounts reduces the risk of dollar loss during periods of inflation and currency devaluation.

Despite the need to maintain low levels of inventory under the above situations, many firms rely heavily on supplies from foreign sources and cannot cut back their purchasing to a great extent. Due to the risk of inflation and the problem of higher prices caused by supply shortages, many firms are developing new purchasing techniques to protect their inventory exposure. Among these are an increased concentration on forecasting of the price and availability of foreign supplies, the negotiation of purchase contracts in hard currencies rather than soft currencies that may inflate, the inclusion of contract revision clauses that would allow price changes within the contract if the price level varies by a certain degree, and the inclusion of escalation clauses that provide for a renegotiation of prices if the exchange rate moves by a certain percentage in either direction. Adherence to such purchasing policies enables the firm to reduce the risk associated with a dependence on foreign supplies as part of its inventory stock and is in consonance with the inventory minimization principle previously stated.

In contrast, firms which import their goods but operate without the restriction of governmental price controls should seek to stockpile inventories in advance of an expected devaluation. The reasoning for this policy is that devaluation at a later date effectively increases the cost of inventory purchases. Again, using the example of a ten percent local currency devaluation, the firm would need to pay ten percent more local currency for the same amount of imported goods from the United States. To avoid this extra cost, a firm could purchase additional quantities of imported materials prior to the anticipated devaluation date. The savings on reduced purchase cost, however, are reduced by increased carrying, insurance, and financing costs. There is, as well, the possibility of increased taxes on a higher level of goods carried. By anticipating the extent of expected devaluation, however, a firm should seek to optimize the amount of inventory stockpiling. We will now examine one particular model that seeks to optimize the level of inventory acquisition by foreign-based subsidiaries operating under inflationary conditions.

The Shapiro Model

Many have recognized the problem of increased inventory cost to firms during periods of declining local currency value. Through the development of a special purchasing model, however, Alan Shapiro provides a means by which companies can elect to either reduce their purchase cost by acquiring advanced stock of inventory or reduce carrying and insurance costs by waiting to purchase until the inventory is actually needed. Shapiro's model first uses the symbols $\lambda\ j, t$ to represent the cost of holding one unit of inventory from the current period j to a future period t. In addition, the total cost of acquisition and holding during this time frame is $p(1 + \lambda\ j, t)$. Secondly, Shapiro's model utilizes an "expected inflation parameter," μ, to predict the degree of inflation from period j to period t. Utilizing this inflation parameter within the framework of a dynamic programming equation, the model is able to determine the minimum expected cost of purchasing one unit of raw material in period t. The decision rule, then, is that the firm will purchase a unit of inventory in period j if the expected cost of buying in period t is greater than the total cost of purchasing in period j (that is, $p(1 + \lambda\ j, t)$. Through this model, Shapiro determined that the firm is "willing to pay a higher and higher price (for inventory) as time goes by if both inflation and the holding cost discount factor are increasing together."[1]

Using the same logic, Shapiro developed a similar dynamic programming equation which indicates the minimum expected cost of inventory purchased in period t given an expected *devaluation* parameter for time period j, t. A firm can thus compute its anticipated inventory cost given a probability of devaluation in addition to conditions of inflation. The key to the effective application of both equations is the ability to forecast inflation rates and devaluation probabilities. This forecasting, unfortunately, is not an easy task at all—as was explained in chapter 3.

Actual Practice

Despite the availability of purchasing models, such as the one described above, as well as the desire for optimization of inventory levels,

[1]Alan Shapiro, "Optimal Inventory and Credit Granting Strategies Under Inflation and Devaluation," *Journal of Financial and Quantitative Analysis*, January 1973, p. 38.

many firms that rely on imported goods persist in maintaining overstocked inventory accounts. As stated in a *Business International* report, "The fears of continued inflation, raw materials shortages, and a number of other environmental constraints . . . are inducing companies to maintain high overseas inventory levels rather than risk curtailment of their overseas operations."[2] The additional environmental constraints include: anticipated import restrictions in foreign countries, anticipated transportation delays caused by dock strikes and slowdowns, the need to maintain intermediate supply centers as worldwide distribution increases, the lack of sophisticated production and inventory control systems abroad necessitating a greater volume of inventory per level of sales, increased difficulty in acquiring foreign exchange for inventory purchases, and the inability to remit funds created by liquidated inventories abroad due to foreign exchange control. From observing the actual inventory policies of MNCs, one can see that as the risk of foreign operations increases, companies are less likely to follow prescribed procedures or optimizing models related to inventory management. Instead, fears of continued shortages and constraints have provoked a suboptimizing buildup of inventories by firms despite the increased financing charges and associated costs of inventory retention.

Pricing

While the discussion so far has centered on preventative measures, such as minimization or stockpiling, that a firm may take to reduce the risk associated with inflationary conditions, additional action can be taken in the area of pricing. During inflationary periods, the foreign firm has two basic policies with respect to price: (a) it can maintain the original price of its inventory in hopes of undercutting competition, or (b) it can increase the price of its inventory in order to at least partially earn the original dollar profit expected. An example will demonstrate the effects of both policies to a firm which has 100 units of imported inventory valued at $200. The original exchange rate was 5X per $1 so the inventory was worth 1,000X. The original cost per unit was 10X and the original selling price was 15X per unit. Assume the foreign currency devalues so that 10X now equals $1.

As shown in Table 5-1, maintenance of the old price will result in a dollar loss on sale of the 100 units even though local figures indicate a profit of 500X. Increasing the price to the dollar equivalent of the original selling price, however, results in a $100 profit.

Adherence to the old selling price results in proceeds which are able to purchase only 75 units at the new cost per unit while following the

[2]"How Inflation, Shortages, Tight Money Affect Global Corporate Inventory Policies," *Business International*, August 30, 1974, p. 273.

TABLE 5-1 Effect of Pricing on Profits

	Policy A: Maintain old price		*Policy B: Adjust price*	
	local currency	dollars (current value)	local currency	dollars (current value)
Sold for	1500X	$150	3000X	$300
Cost*	1000X	200	1000X	200
Profit	500X	($50)	2000X	$100

*CGS translated at historic rate.

selling price increase of Policy B actually allows for an increase in inventory level to 150 units by reinvesting the revenue generated from sales at the new price. Of course a price rise of the magnitude indicated in Policy B would probably discourage some sales, but a certain level of increase is nonetheless required if the firm wants to prevent a deterioration of converted earnings. In general, firms should price their inventory goods in such a manner as to consider replacement costs of these goods rather than their historic costs.

Summary

In summary, MNCs must manage inventory differently than domestic firms. More complex variables come into play because of many different environments. The subsidiaries are operating under many changing and different governmental tax and control regulations. Prices and exchange rates are constantly altering the resultant profit margins also.

Multinational corporations, therefore, should have inventory management policies which reflect these changing conditions. It is essential for these firms to have an internationally oriented system for determining the appropriate level of inventory at each subsidiary and to maintain a flexible pricing policy in order to take advantage of local opportunities and reduce dollar losses due to inflation or currency devaluation.

Bibliography

Business International. "How Inflation, Shortages, Tight Money Affect Global Corporate Inventory Policies." *Business International,* August 30, 1974, p. 273.

Eiteman, David, and Arthur Stonehill, *Multinational Business Finance.* Reading, Mass.: Addison-Wesley Publishing Company, Inc., 1973, pp. 303–7.

Shapiro, Alan. "Optimal Inventory and Credit Granting Strategies Under Inflation and Devaluation." *Journal of Financial and Quantitative Analysis,* January 1973, p. 38.

Part Three

CAPITAL BUDGETING AND CONTROL

6

Capital Budgeting*

CAPITAL budgeting in the multinational firm involves several new environmental aspects not encountered by the domestic firm. The financial manager should no longer view only the domestic sources and potential investments of funds, but must now include all the international fund sources and potential investments as well. To cover for their lack of analysis in the international realm of business, many managers use the excuse that "traditional financial analysis tools don't apply." This is not actually the case. The same financial methods still apply, but in the multinational corporation they must be used in the context of many environments. The new environments will have many dissimilar financial attitudes, dissimilar financial institutions and instruments, dissimilar legal systems, dissimilar government types and policies, and a host of other pertinent differences.

It should be observed that capital budgeting in a multinational firm involves the same techniques that a uninational firm would use, but these techniques must be applied in conjunction with a careful consideration of the many additional variables, risks, and constraints inherent in the multinational environment. Before an intelligent capital budgeting decision can be made, these additional factors should all be

*Most of the material in this chapter was originally published by the author and Stanley R. Jewell in the *Atlanta Economic Review*, November-December 1973, p. 4.

considered, and the international financial manager should have at least some knowledge of the ways he may reduce, or shift, these new risks (as noted in chapter 1). This chapter deals with the more directly related problems of capital budgeting in multinational business.

The Appropriate Cost of Capital (COC)

The first unique problem to be examined concerns the decision to use the domestic cost of capital only, the foreign capital market cost of capital only, or some weighted average of the two. In general, if a firm's capital is obtained only overseas, only the foreign cost of capital is used. If a firm's capital is obtained only domestically, only the domestic cost of capital should be used (determined by the same techniques as are applicable to the uninational firm). In most cases, however, the multinational firm employs centralized financing using the whole world as a combined source of funds, and the appropriate cost of capital is an overall weighted average. This is determined as shown below:

$$\left(\begin{array}{l}\text{\% of total company's}\\ \text{capital obtained in}\\ \text{a particular country}\\ \text{from a particular}\\ \text{source}\end{array}\right) \times \left(\begin{array}{l}\text{\% cost of}\\ \text{that capital}\\ \text{from that}\\ \text{country and}\\ \text{source}\end{array}\right) = \left(\begin{array}{l}\text{Contribution to}\\ \text{total weighted}\\ \text{average COC}\\ \text{by that partic-}\\ \text{ular source}\end{array}\right)$$

Then:

$$\left(\begin{array}{l}\text{All contributions}\\ \text{to total weighted}\\ \text{average COC from}\\ \text{various sources}\end{array}\right) = \left(\begin{array}{l}\text{Total weighted}\\ \text{average COC}\\ \text{for the company}\end{array}\right)$$

Using domestic COC figures only, a multinational firm might accept a project returning nine percent because its domestic COC is eight percent. But overseas funds might cost twelve percent and the global COC might be ten percent for this firm. Such a firm would be accepting projects with returns that are obviously below its global COC if it considered only its domestic COC.

Sometimes a multinational firm only considers its COC in the particular nation where the proposed project is to operate. Such a firm is usually making several serious errors. It is assuming that the project has no effect whatsoever outside that nation, and that local costs and returns are independent of the costs and returns of the firm elsewhere. Obviously, such is seldom the case. The parent company usually affects the subsidiary's abilities and costs in raising capital and making returns on it. It is just no longer economically rational to think of each subsidiary as being totally independent. Local projects and their costs must be evaluated on a global basis.

Risk Absorption

A second area to be considered briefly is that of uncertainty absorption. How will all the risks, constraints, and new variables that occur when investing overseas be quantified and absorbed in the capital budgeting process, and what will this process actually be?

The first possibility usually presented is that of accounting for the new risks by using a discount rate uniformly higher than the firm's weighted average COC. The first problem with this method is that it makes no allowance for the time pattern of uncertainty. If an investment's returns are highly uncertain in the near future, it is unlikely that it should be accepted at all. If the uncertainties are primarily in the more distant future, the above method would penalize for uncertainty too heavily the early cash flows, and would not sufficiently penalize the distant cash flows. The other major problem of the method described here is that there is no allowance made for the actual dollar amounts at risk. Different reinvestment and financing policies would have different amounts of uncovered dollar investment open for loss.

Stonehill and Nathanson have presented an excellent capital budgeting method that allows for the incorporation of all the new risks and a systematic evaluation of investment alternatives. The technique allows for uncertainty in the multinational firm by charging against "each period's incremental cash flows the cost of a program of uncertainty absorption for that period, whether or not the program was actually undertaken."[1] In determining the incremental cash flows for a period, one would include in cash inflows to the parent firm such items as net dividends paid to the parent company, net payments to the parent company of management contracts, license fees, royalties, disclosure fees, net loan repayments and interest, and the "cash-out" or market value of the subsidiary at the time horizon. The cash outflows would include all capital transfers, loans, etc., to the subsidiary firm.

Whether or not the cost of a particular "insurance program" against risk is considered, the charge for uncertainty absorption depends on whether the insurance program costs more than or less than the reduction in the expected value of loss achieved by the program. If the reduction in expected loss is less than the cost of the corresponding insurance program, the expected loss due to the risks should be con-

[1]Arthur Stonehill and L. Nathanson, "Capital Budgeting and Multinational Companies," *California Management Review*, Summer 1968, p. 46.

sidered the charge for uncertainty absorption, and vice versa. The potential losses are reduced to an expected value by assuming a probability distribution of various types of risks. In the case of complete uncertainty, the cost of insurance should be a fair estimate for the expected value of the loss.

Once the lesser net cost of either the risk insurance program or the corresponding expected loss due to sustaining the risk for a period—the lesser value is the cost of uncertainty absorption—is determined and charged against the net incremental cash flows for the period, the capital budgeting decision is essentially solved. The firm should make those capital investments that provide the highest net incremental cash inflows for the period being considered. The chosen technique has, therefore, avoided a direct calculation of the effects of the risks on the firm's COC, but instead has accounted for the risks by altering the firm's incremental cash flows.

Differing National Tax Jurisdictions

Capital budgeting solutions must also take taxation into consideration. This is where the problems become complex. Actually, the unique issue here is whether or not to evaluate all investment opportunities after all income taxes have been deducted even though part of the tax is due only when funds are repatriated from the subsidiary. Assume, for example, that the income tax rate in the country of the parent company is sixty percent, but that profits are taxed only at forty percent where earned, with another tax of twenty percent levied on repatriated profits. Suppose that an investment with an eight percent return is available to the subsidiary, and one returning ten percent is available to the parent company. For a pretax income of $100 in the subsidiary, the local investment would yield $.08 \times \$60 = \$4.80$, and the domestic investment would yield $.10 \times \$40 = \$4.00$. Thus, it would be preferable to retain the profits in the subsidiary not only in terms of income, but also because retention in the subsidiary would give a greater net worth for a consolidated company if no reserve were set up for the subsequent incremental tax in the country of the parent.[2]

There are several possible treatments of the incremental tax on repatriated earnings. The first involves the practice of always reducing the subsidiary earnings immediately by the amount of the incremental tax. This technique is favorable to those who believe the ultimate purpose of all earnings is to return to the parent company. It regards all the funds from all operations as a single pool, and the eight percent

[2]For an expanded discussion of this concept see Dan Smith, "Financial Variables in International Business," *Harvard Business Review*, January-February 1966, pp. 94–97.

local investment illustrated in the example just given would never be preferable to the ten percent domestic investment.

Another possible way of treating the incremental tax on repatriated earnings is to not reduce the subsidiary earnings at all with respect to the incremental tax. This is really a multinational view where each unit of the company is considered equally important. No subsidiary, or the parent, is less an integral part of the overall operation than the other, and thus investment decisions would only be distorted if the incremental tax were taken into effect.

The third situation is the case where the incremental tax is considered only on the portion of the subsidiary's earnings expected to be repatriated. Thus, the overall tax rate for the firm is actually a combination of the "where earned" tax and the "repatriated" tax. This "weighted average" tax is not, however, directly applicable to any particular source of income since it would not be the correct tax for any individual income source. Using this alternative, most firms set up a reserve to cover the potential tax on subsidiary earnings not yet repatriated. Since this reserve is regarded as a liability, the net worth of the company will not be increased simply because funds are left abroad. This approach appears to be more realistic and should lead to investment decisions that maximize earnings and available funds.[3]

Another very important tax-related factor in capital budgeting is the use of "tax havens." Prior to the 1962 Revenue Act, earnings of subsidiaries were not taxed until they were repatriated to the parent company in the United States. Earnings of branches, however, were subject to United States taxes whether repatriated or not. Almost all firms had established tax haven subsidiaries—sales and holding companies, in effect—in countries with low tax rates. All foreign earnings were then funneled through these tax havens in order to take advantage of the tax-deferral privilege. Reinvestments in foreign opportunities were made from these subsidiaries without the earnings ever returning to the United States and being taxed. Under the rules of the 1962 Revenue Act, however, the parent company of these tax haven subsidiaries may be subject to United States taxes on undistributed income from certain activities and may be "deemed" to have received a dividend subject to United States taxes.[4]

In addition to considering statutory tax differentials, the multinational firm must also view the "effective" tax rates confronting it. Investment credits, grants of tax relief on investments favored by the government, special allowances for inventory reserves, etc., all create a spread between the actual and effective tax rates. Obviously, tax experts should be consulted to determine all the intricacies of tax laws.

The problems of transfer pricing are also very important tax-related

---

[3] *Ibid.*, p. 97.

[4] *Information Guide for U.S. Corporations Doing Business Abroad* (New York: Price Waterhouse & Co., January 1972).

challenges of the financial manager. Transfer pricing sometimes alters the prices of products and materials for the purpose of gaining a tax advantage or for de facto profit repatriation. By ignoring any sort of value-added concept and artificially establishing transfer prices, a company can adjust its earnings to appear in the countries with lower tax rates. In a like manner, it can effectively shift profits from one country to another, or repatriate them to the parent company (especially useful if the host country has clamped down on dividend remission). There are many problems involved here, however. The primary ones are the internal friction generated when profit-oriented performance measures are used even though profits are shifted by top corporate management, and the possibility of government retaliation or regulation in some manner.

Investments in Less-Developed Countries (LDCs)

The special question of evaluating investment opportunities in less-developed countries has been avoided until now because of certain unique characteristics involved. In general, the same sort of capital budgeting techniques and considerations apply here as have been described throughout this chapter. The characteristics that need to be noted now are certain forms of substantial risk, of investment sources and guaranties, and of acceptance criteria unique to, or at least more critical to, evaluating investments in LDCs.

Conversion risks relating to a country's changes in exchange rates are more frequently encountered in LDCs, but a far more important risk in the LDC is the expropriation risk pertaining to the absolute safety and profitability of a foreign venture per se. Whereas the conversion risk can at least be tolerated, the expropriation risk, if it materializes, cannot. The expropriation risk—a function of the political, military, and economic developments in the LDC directly related to the particular investment—is probably the greatest single obstacle to international capital flows in the LDC today.[5]

The expropriation risk varies inversely with an investor's ability to demonstrate that the cost/benefit ratios for his investment are more attractive than any other alternative which offers approximately equivalent benefits. Not only is it unrealistic to use a presumption of general net economic advantage to a host country to justify foreign direct investment, but the foreign investor must always view his investment as being constantly "on trial" against other investment alternatives available to the host country.

It seems reasonable that, because the risks involved are high, an

[5]Peter Gabriel, "The Investment in the LDC: Asset with a Fixed Maturity," *Columbia Journal of World Business*, Summer 1966, p. 116.

investment in an LDC should be considered somewhat of a "fixed maturity" investment; that is, the nature and magnitude of the resource allocation should be balanced against the time span for which returns can "safely" be expected. Conditions which would allow the investor to control and expand the applicable time span are: (1) the uniqueness to the *firm* of the particular skills and technology which the investment introduces into the LDC; (2) the degree to which these resources are critical to the efficient operation of the enterprise created in the LDC; (3) the degree to which the continuous application of intrafirm research and development prevents the weakening of the investor's initial leadership position due to the "obligations" (perceived by the host government) to spread the firm's technology within the LDC.[6] To prevent the host government from succumbing to the pressure of nationalistic charges that the foreign investor has outlived his usefulness, the foreign investor must make his contribution evident both with a continuous stream of valuable innovations, and with benefits to the host country's balance-of-payments situation and real national income growth. The investor in the LDC will usually see his benefits falling and his costs rising from the very start of his investment.

Investors in LDCs are also faced with a variety of financing alternatives largely outside the sphere of normal capital markets. The LDCs generally have no free, efficient, and broadly based capital markets. Artificial credit rationing and artificial restriction or regulation on the permissible types of investments are common. But there are many private international and intergovernmental financing agencies —for example, Edge Act corporations, the U.S. Agency for International Development (AID), Export-Import Bank, International Finance Corporation (IFC), and the Inter-American Development Bank (IDB). All of these agencies will make loans to worthwhile private businesses in LDCs where these loans are believed to be directly aiding the growth of the local economy as well as stimulating direct foreign investment. In general, the financing terms available from these agencies are more lenient than those found in the local private capital markets—in order to induce private investment toward priority investment areas. Subsidized financing does, therefore, become a major consideration in evaluating investment in LDCs.

Summary and Conclusions

This chapter has introduced the major problems of capital budgeting in multinational firms. In particular, problems related to determining the appropriate cost of capital, accounting for additional risks,

[6]*Ibid.*, p. 117.

and handling additional tax regulations have been at least partially examined—with respect to doing business both in major industrial countries and in the less developed nations.

It is concluded that somewhat different approaches should be used in evaluating investments in LDCs and evaluating investments in developed countries. In LDCs, instead of approaching the cost-of-capital problem by surveying the required rate of return, the financial manager must look for those particular investment opportunities where he may obtain subsidized development financing. The cutoff rate of return for investments in LDCs is viewed differently because of the close connection between the sources and uses of funds. Projects that fall short of a market COC test may suddenly appear quite profitable when the financing is obtained on favorable nonmarket terms. Therefore, in the LDC, the financing decision actually tends to precede the investment decision, which is the converse of the situation in developed economies. When discussing investments in less-developed countries, the financial manager who maximizes the return for his shareholders is usually the manager aware that certain sources of financing may be open to him only if he expands into those areas whose development is most favored by the host government. In addition to being aware of the many sources of funds available from the various international and intergovernmental agencies, the financial manager must also consider the numerous investment guaranties and insurance programs offered by these agencies—for example, the specific risk guaranties, extended risk guaranties, and housing guaranties offered by such agencies as AID.

Bibliography

Adler, Michael. "Cost of Capital and Valuation of a Two-Country Firm." *Journal of Finance,* March 1974, pp. 119–32.

———, and Bernard Dumas, "Optimal International Acquisitions." *Journal of Finance,* March 1975, pp. 1–19.

Aharoni, Yair. *The Foreign Investment Decision Process.* Boston, Mass.: Harvard Graduate School of Business Administration, Division of Research, 1966.

Carter, Eugene. *Portfolio Aspects of Corporate Capital Budgets.* Boston, Mass.: D. C. Heath and Company, 1974.

Cohn, Richard, and John Pringle, "Imperfections in International Financial Markets: Implications for Risk Premia and the Cost of Capital to Firms." *Journal of Finance,* March 1973, pp. 59–66.

Eiteman, David, and Arthur Stonehill, *Multinaitonal Business Finance.* Reading, Mass.: Addison-Wesley Publishing Company, Inc., 1973. pp. 189–227.

Foster, Earl. "The Impact of Inflation on Capital Budgeting Decisions." *Quarterly Review of Economics and Business,* Autumn 1970, pp. 19–24.

Gabriel, Peter. "The Investment in the LDC: Asset with a Fixed Maturity." *Columbia Journal of World Business,* Summer 1966, pp. 109–89.

Gaddis, Paul. "Analyzing Overseas Investments." *Harvard Business Review,* May-June 1966, pp. 115–22.

Green, Robert, and William Cunningham, "The Determinants of U.S. Foreign Investments: An Empirical Examination." *Management International Review* 15 (no. 2–3, 1975): 113–20.

Kohers, Theodor. "The Effect of Multinational Operations on the Cost of Equity Capital of U.S. Corporations: An Empirical Study." *Management International Review* 15 (no. 2–3, 1975): 121–24.

Levy, Haim, and Marshall Sarnat, "International Diversification of Investment Portfolios." *American Economic Review,* September 1970, pp. 668–75.

Mehta, Dileep. "Capital Budgeting Procedures for a Multinational Firm." In *Management of the Multinationals,* edited by Seth and Holton, pp. 271–91. New York: The Free Press, 1974.

Nehrt, Lee. *International Finance for Multinational Corporations,* 2nd ed. Scranton, Pa.: Intext, Inc., 1972. pp. 465–535.

Piper, James. "How U.S. Firms Evaluate Foreign Investment Opportunities." *MSU Business Topics,* Summer 1971, pp. 11–20.

Ricks, David, and Stanley Jewell, "Capital Budgeting Problems in Companies with Internationally Distributed Investments." *Atlanta Economic Review,* November-December 1973, pp. 4–7.

Rodriguez, Rita, and Eugene Carter, *International Financial Management.* Englewood Cliffs, N.J.: Prentice-Hall, Inc., 1976. pp. 324–441.

Stevens, G. V. G. "Fixed Investment Expenditures of Foreign Manufacturing Affiliates of U.S. Firms: Theoretical Models and Empirical Evidence." *Yale Economic Essays,* Spring 1969, pp. 136–93.

Stobaugh, Robert B., Jr. "How to Analyze Foreign Investment Climates." *Harvard Business Review,* September-October 1969, pp. 100–108.

———. "Where in the World Should We Put that Plant." *Harvard Business Review,* January-February 1969, pp. 129–36.

Stonehill, Arthur, and L. Nathanson, "Capital Budgeting and Multinational Companies." *California Management Review,* Summer 1968, pp. 39–54.

Treuherz, Rolf. "Re-Evaluating ROI for Foreign Operations." *Financial Executive,* May 1968, pp. 65–71.

Weston, J. Fred, and Bart W. Sorge, *International Managerial .Finance.* Homewood, Ill.: Richard D. Irwin, 1972, pp. 208–33.

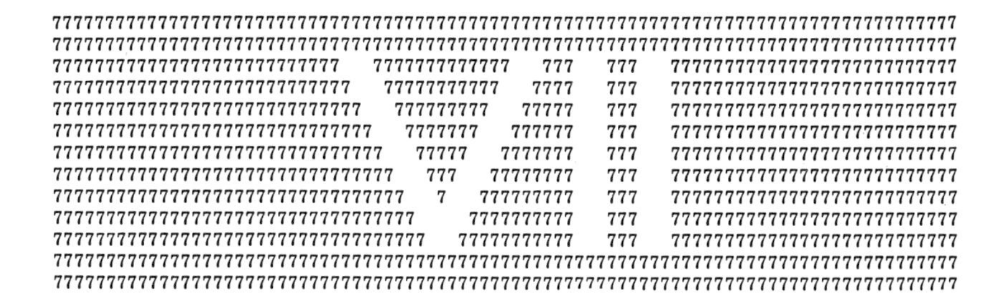

Financial Control Systems

MOST growing firms become increasingly difficult to manage. This certainly has been true for most of the companies that have expanded by going overseas.

One of the most complex international additions to management problems has been in the field of financial control so we will begin by briefly examining the general concept of financial control of subsidiaries. Then we will survey the influences unique to the multinational firm that must be considered in the design and utilization of its financial control system. Finally, we will consider and make some recommendations regarding three major areas of concern to the international financial manager: (1) the requirements for an optimally effective financial model of the multinational corporation, (2) the relative merits of return on investment and residual income as management performance measurement methods, and (3) methods of ameliorating the performance-distorting effects of headquarters-directed transfer pricing between subsidiaries.

The Basic Concept

A financial control system (FCS) for firms with subsidiaries must perform three basic functions: (1) set objectives mutually agreeable to subsidiary and parent managements, (2) measure results of operations, and (3) analyze operational variances and evaluate subsidiary managements.[1]

In setting objectives, the system should provide for the participation of all parties who will be using the plan to ensure as complete an information flow as possible at this stage and to facilitate future communications regarding the plan. Plans must also be critically examined to optimize goal congruence. Finally, the performance criteria must be clear and agreeable to all concerned.

When reporting, the system must provide for reports in the same general format and the same units as are given in the budget to facilitate effective and efficient comparison of planned and actual performance. Deviations from the plan should be subject to variance analysis (to determine what caused the variation), evaluation [to assess the significance of the causal factor(s)], and projection, if indicated, of the variance(s) into the relevant future period(s). Conclusions of variance analysis should be reflected, to the extent applicable, in the evaluation of subsidiary management performance.

International Dimensions

There are three major types of international influences on the FCS: (1) those affecting financial statements, (2) those related to operating and financial risks, and (3) influences on FCS administration which are nonquantifiable.[2]

Financial Statements

Considerations such as currency valuation changes, inflation, and taxes of all sorts may have relatively minor operational effects but can change the income statement from black to red when stated in the currency of the parent company. Consideration of all these factors is essential to the technical design of an effective FCS.

For an FCS to function effectively in an environment of various and unstable currencies, some common ground for the measurement of management results is essential. Objectives and results should be communicated in terms of a single currency (usually that of the parent company's headquarters) to permit easier evaluation and comparison of subsidiary management results. To an American parent company the relevant short-term information is not usually how many cruzeiros

[1]Herbert C. Knortz, "Controllership in International Corporations," *Financial Executive*, June 1969, pp. 54–60.

[2]Edward C. Bursk, John Dearden, David F. Hawkins, and Victor M. Longstreet, *Financial Control of Multinational Operations* (New York: Financial Executives Research Foundation, 1971), p. 38.

its Brazilian subsidiary has earned, but how many dollars they are worth. Such a policy tends to motivate the subsidiary manager to take necessary actions to enhance the parent company's financial condition despite currency valuation changes and to note the relevant variables in his periodic reports. As this implies, the overseas subsidiary manager must exhibit a wider spectrum of knowledge and abilities than an otherwise comparable domestic manager.

Operating and Financial Risks

A second major class of influences on the MNC's control system is related to operating and financial risks. These risks include: (1) exchange controls, (2) expropriation, (3) political instability, (4) governmental regulations, (5) import-export controls, and (6) limited and/or more costly local credit. Because of their significance, such risks must be accounted for in the setting of performance standards, operating policies, and capital investment proposal evaluations.

Nonquantifiable Aspects

The third group of influences, the nonquantitative factors, are particularly important in the larger MNC with operations dispersed about the globe since policy, cost considerations, and local political considerations usually dictate extensive, if not complete, use of local nationals for operations in each country. Use of local citizens in financial management posts may have profound effects on the FCS administration since personal value systems, cultural backgrounds, and educational levels around the world will differ markedly. One partial solution to this problem is to give local managers a period of orientation and training at the parent company headquarters, and to maintain frequent personal communications subsequent to this training to reinforce its effects.

An MNC usually will have subsidiaries in several environments and at several stages of maturity. Accordingly, the parent management's views of the various budgets should cover the entire spectrum from pure forecast to pure commitment, and allow for the differences in each environment.

Whatever the appropriate view of the budget, it should be noted that each subsidiary needs to include some sort of forecast or early warning system.

The increased risks inherent in business operations in more than one environment accentuate the need for the FCS to provide advance warning of significant environmental changes. Traditional financial control systems are essentially historical in nature and ineffectual predictors of the future. The most effective source of information regarding current trends in an environment usually is a man who is alert and functioning in that environment. Accordingly, the recommended FCS should include a requirement that, with each periodic report on operations (or as often as needed), the subsidiary manager must submit a brief report on environmental changes and trends with an estimate as to their probable effect(s) on the level and profitability of his operations. The essentiality and utility of this report will tend to be directly proportional to the rapidity of environmental change and inversely proportional to the age of the subsidiary.[3]

Additional Problems

Top management may view the budget in two different ways: they may consider the budget either as a forecast or as a commitment. Each of these viewpoints is entirely functional in some environments and extremely dysfunctional in others, so both might well be used simultaneously by an MNC for controlling different subsidiaries.

FORECAST VS. COMMITMENT

When the budget is perceived as a forecast or prediction of what is expected, it is a most effective communication tool, representing the subsidiary manager's best estimate of what is most likely to occur in the coming period. Naturally, accurate estimates are preferred but, as conditions change significantly, the forecast can be changed concurrently to reflect the revised prospects (including with the change notice, of course, an explanation of the events that necessitated the change). Under this conceptualization of the budget, a separate performance measurement is needed unless top management can subjectively evaluate the manager's performance adequately (a practice which is seldom recommended). The forecast budget is most used and most effective in environments featuring rapid change, either of product development or of other aspects of the external environment (such as political, currency, or inflation instability), and is representative of the Theory Y school of personnel management (which is characterized by delegation of authority).

The Theory X practitioner, however, typically makes more decisions himself and views meeting or surpassing the budget as an implicit obligation of the subsidiary manager. Consequently, the average manager tends to be conservative in his profit estimates, padding whenever possible, since there is seldom a budgeted reserve for contingencies and the budgeted profit exhibits a strong tendency to be fixed throughout the period. This method tends to inhibit communications

[3] *Ibid.*, pp. 14–15.

because the subsidiary manager is motivated to conceal mistakes or misfortunes as long as possible in the hope of some unforeseen fortuitous event occurring to restore his operation to budgeted profit levels.

Viewing the budget as a commitment requires extremely accurate predictions of all relevant variables and frequent comprehensive reporting. This view of the budget is most effective in operations with a short time span in older, more stable subsidiaries where the currency changes, if any, are predictable with a high degree of confidence. It requires, also, that the headquarters staff have an intimate knowledge of the subsidiary's total environment.

ROI VS. RESIDUAL INCOME

Another problem that becomes even more complex for MNCs concerns the question of whether to use return on investment (ROI) or the residual income approach to evaluation of control. ROI, however measured, is a popular statistic for most companies, both in the macro- and micro-evaluation of management. Claims made for ROI include the following: (1) It is a summary of all influences operating on the area delineated as the responsibility of the manager in question, whether he be the company's chief executive or its lowest foreman; (2) it measures the effectiveness of property utilization; (3) it facilitates direct comparison of subsidiaries and other investments; and (4) it can be easily calculated from available accounting data.[4]

Residual income has not yet been widely accepted, possibly because its effective use requires advance preparation. It cannot be computed as simply as ROI (by dividing one income statement figure by one balance sheet figure). The concept behind the residual income approach to profit evaluation is that different types of assets have different inherent risks and are affected in different ways by environmental changes. Accordingly, residual income advocates hold that different returns (proportionate to the totality of relevant risks) should be required from different assets, or from the same assets in different environments. This approach has great intuitive appeal, since holding cash in a country with a fifty percent annual inflation rate is obviously riskier than holding cash in countries having low inflation rates. Effective use of the residual income approach would require that managements (1) determine the relevant rates of return required from each type of asset in each environment, and (2) compute the total return (in dollars or the currency of the parent company) required for each unit by multiplying the return (percent) required for each asset by the budgeted average balance sheet value for that asset and summing

[4]Charles T. Horngren, *Cost Accounting: A Managerial Emphasis* (Englewood Cliffs, N.J.: Prentice-Hall, Inc., 1972), pp. 691–717.

these to get the total budgeted return. The amount of net income earned beyond this target would be the residual income. Subsidiaries could be evaluated more fairly by comparing absolute residual incomes earned (if their initial income requirements were very similar) or by comparing the percentages over 100 percent.

Recommendations

Given the additional and unique multinational FCS problems just discussed, we now need to consider more completely what should be done about them. In this final section we will describe ideals of the MNC, recommend a performance measurement, and present a brief discussion on effective management of intersubsidiary transactions.

A Financial Model of the MNC

An optimally effective FCS for a large MNC must be designed as though domestic operations are just a subset of worldwide operations warranting only attention proportionate to their relative size, profitability, risks, and opportunities. This implies that if an MNC is to develop and use a financial model, then that model must be designed to accommodate the full range of factors which are operative or likely to be operative in the MNC's relevant world (those countries where the MNC is operating or likely to operate before scheduled revision of the financial model).

Construction of this model would entail explicit consideration of all relevant factors and their interrelationships. Admittedly, such a model would be extremely complex, but, if the construction were sufficiently well researched and interrelationships were painstakingly quantified, the resultant model would be an invaluable aid to financial managers. They would no longer have to make so many subjective estimates of the effects of a given change, but could "plug" the expected change into the model and determine the effects that would ensue. For example, it would permit rapid recognition of the total effects of a ten percent devaluation of the dollar on parent company balance sheets and income statements, thus enabling financial personnel to determine what measures, if any, should be taken to ameliorate the unfavorable effects or enhance the favorable effects of such an eventuality, given the likelihood of its occurrence.

Performance Measurement Method

Operating on a global basis as recommended is much easier in theory than in practice. One of the most complex control problems the financial manager will face concerns performance evaluation. As mentioned earlier, there are two major types of performance measurement methods: ROI and residual income. ROI is the one most commonly used at present, but residual income is the most conceptually attractive. ROI is too simplistic for effective use in the MNC. It ignores many relevant variables and consistently points toward acceptance of high risks. It also assumes implicitly that all assets within an environment are subject to the same risks, an assumption that may often be invalid. Furthermore, the determination of what figure to use for "investment" in the ROI computation can virtually dictate the type of suboptimal behavior the ambitious manager will engage in.

The two most common "investment" figures used in ROI computations are net book value and gross book value. Given the same physical assets, net book value decreases annually as plant and equipment depreciate. The manager with fully depreciated equipment will tend to retain it as long as he can net more than variable costs from its operation. Similarly, he will be dissuaded from investing in new or replacement equipment longer than is economically justifiable due to the relatively much higher net book value on new equipment.

Gross book value as an investment base has the opposite disadvantages. Since the investment base does *not* decrease with time, the ambitious manager can improve his ROI by scrapping useful assets that are beginning to require nonroutine maintenance in favor of new ones that are slightly more efficient. The result may be uneconomically rapid fixed asset replacement.

A third "investment" value is available for use in ROI computations, and it is more acceptable than either of the other two. It uses market values or a reasonable facsimile thereof. As would be expected, this value is more difficult and expensive to use than either of the above, since the data, unlike gross and net book value, are not readily available from the accounting function. When used, however, it does avoid the extreme operational disadvantages cited for net and gross book values.

A further disadvantage of ROI is that its use in a profit measurement system is inconsistent with the usual techniques used in capital investment analysis. Profit measurement usually entails straight line or accelerated depreciation (for tax purposes), net book value, and after-tax profits. But investment analysis usually employs discounted net cash flows. A depreciation rate computed from annuity tables can overcome this discrepancy if and only if the cash flows are constant and even. In the real world this requirement is rarely if ever satisfied, so annuity depreciation is rarely used even though it is theoretically desirable from a goal congruence standpoint in a theoretical world of regular, equal annual cash flows.

Residual income, on the other hand, involves the setting of absolute profit objectives for each unit based on the amounts of each type of asset within the unit and the assets' vulnerability to the recognized environmental risks within which the unit operates. This method of performance measurement permits incorporation of judgment into return requirements for various assets, so the disadvantages of using book value of plant and equipment may be largely offset by subjectively adjusting the rate of return required from fixed assets, depending on the extent to which top management wants to encourage or discourage modernization of plant and equipment. Although residual income has the advantages mentioned earlier and the flexibility just noted, and is capable of producing goal congruence and facilitating comparison of operating effectiveness between subsidiaries, its use cannot affect evaluation of actual results from a particular investment within a unit unless this investment is significant enough to be designated a profit center in its own right. Accordingly, management performance must generally be evaluated after the fact and investment decisions must be made on best estimates of projected cash flows with limited follow-up opportunities.

Intersubsidiary Transactions

Operating on a global basis, as recommended, also creates the opportunity to choose where many risks are faced. In fact, a commonly used method of reducing the aggregate of risks faced by the MNC is the utilization of a variant of the insurance principle: instead of having only one large manufacturing plant that produces exports to many countries, the prudent MNC produces components or entire end products in many countries, thus limiting the assets exposed to instability of a single currency or government. As a consequence, the average size of an MNC's subsidiary tends to be only a small proportion of total MNC assets. Moreover, functions of subsidiaries tend to be specialized; a few are in manufacturing and most are in marketing. Such a structure results in a relatively large volume of transfers between subsidiaries. This relationship usually presents the subsidiary marketing organization with a fixed transfer price and may distort the total reported variable costs of production incurred by the MNC as a whole, possibly resulting in less than optimal subsidiary marketing policies.[5] But alternative corrective actions to reduce the dysfunctional effect of a single fixed transfer price are possible.

One possibility is to establish a two-part price for transfers. Under this procedure (1) the buying unit would estimate annual requirements for each product, and (2) the selling unit would (a) determine

---

[5]James M. Shulman, "When the Price is Wrong—By Design," *Columbia Journal of World Business*, May-June 1967, pp. 69–76.

amount and types of assets required to support these requirements, and (b) bill the buying unit on a periodic basis for the fixed costs (including profit) those reserved assets should earn and the standard variable costs per unit actually required. This two-part price would not only ameliorate the dysfunctional effect of normal transfer pricing just described but, furthermore, would motivate the buying unit to purchase at least as many units as projected, since its effective unit cost would decrease to that point and would tend to stabilize the selling unit's profit expectations. A variety of controls might be specified to preclude the buying unit's manager from projecting an unrealistically low level of sales.

The second major possibility is that of measuring a marketing unit's performance in terms of the total contribution earned over variable costs (marketing and manufacturing). Under this method, the producing unit's manager would be evaluated on his actual costs relative to mutually acceptable (between parent and subsidiary) standard costs. Use of this method would necessarily entail maintenance of an additional set of books unless both operations were within a single corporation in one country, since a fair percentage of the profits would have to be attributed to the producing unit to allow computation of local income taxes. (In both of the above alternatives, of course, the variable costs would necessarily include any applicable taxes or duties.)

When manipulation of transfer prices by headquarters personnel is possible, although it may result in greater benefits than costs (direct and imputed) worldwide, it may distort the reported profitability of affected subsidiaries. To compensate for this effect, normal budgets (using economically realistic transfer prices) should be constructed, adjusted to account for the variations produced by transfer price changes, and used as actual operating budgets by subsidiary managers. This same derived budget should also be used to evaluate subsidiary management performance. In short, one of the possible corrective actions just described or some similar system of information dissemination should be employed to prevent artificial transfer prices from causing misguided decisions.

Bibliography

Bursk, Edward, John Dearden, David Hawkins, and Victor Longstreet. *Financial Control of Multinational Operations.* New York: Financial Executives Research Foundation, 1971.

Eiteman, David and Arthur Stonehill, *Multinational Business Finance.* Reading, Mass.: Addison-Wesley Publishing Company, Inc., 1973. pp. 343–67.

Farag, Shawki. "The Problem of Performance Evaluation in International Accounting." *International Journal of Accounting,* Fall 1974, pp. 45–53.

Imdieke, Leroy, and Charles Smith. "International Financial Control Problems and the Accounting Control System." *Management International Review,* no. 4–5, 1975, p. 13.

Knortz, Herbert. "Controllership in International Corporations." *Financial Executive,* June 1969, pp. 54–60.

Mauriel, John. "Evaluation and Control of Overseas Operations." *Management Accounting,* May 1969, pp. 35–39.

Meister, Irene. *Managing the International Financial Function.* New York: The National Industrial Conference Board, 1970.

Mueller, G. *International Accounting.* New York: The Macmillan Company, 1967.

Nehrt, Lee. *International Finance for Multinational Business,* 2nd ed. Scranton, Pa.: Intext, Inc., 1972. pp. 659–710.

Robbins, Sidney, and Robert Stobaugh, "The Bent Measuring Stick for Foreign Subsidiaries." *Harvard Business Review,* September-October 1976, p. 80.

Rodney, Earl. "Financial Controls for Multinational Operations." *Financial Executive,* May 1976, pp. 26–28.

Scott, George. "Information Systems and Coordination in Multinational Enterprise." *International Journal of Accounting,* Fall 1974, pp. 87–105.

Shulman, James. "When the Price is Wrong—By Design." *Columbia Journal of World Business,* May-June 1967, pp. 69–76.

Part Four

FINANCING BUSINESS OPERATIONS

VIII

Capital Structure

Theory

THERE are basically two theoretical schools of thought concerning the proportion of debt to equity financing that should be used in the corporation.

Very briefly, the Modigliani-Miller school holds that two firms of the same industry, offering identical sets of assets, should not have different overall market values (or costs of capital) by varying the amount of financial leverage in each firm. Allowing for bankruptcy costs and the tax advantage of debt financing, a potential change in the cost of capital provided by a change in the cost of debt financing would be offset by a simultaneous change in the opposite direction of the cost of equity financing. Many believe that this theory is correct, but only under such simplifying assumptions as a perfect capital market.

The other view, known as the traditional view, holds that there are three general ranges of market value (or cost of capital) associated with increasing degrees of financial leverage. For increasing but still low degrees, the market value rises (concurrently, the cost of capital falls). Over the next few degrees, the market value stabilizes (the cost of capital does also). This is referred to as the theoretically optimal range of financial leverage. Finally, past a high point of leverage, the market value declines (and the cost of capital increases).

Research Findings

In a study of United States multinational corporations and their subsidiaries by Robert Leftwich, it was determined that the cost of capital does not necessarily rise with increasing and high degrees of financial leverage for the subsidiary (contrary to the conclusions of the traditional view).[1] In a sample of some 298 United States parent corporations and their 5,237 subsidiaries, Leftwich found the subsidiaries to have higher degrees of financial leverage than the United States parents (approximately twenty-eight percent higher).

According to the traditional view, past a certain point of financial leverage, the cost of capital usually rises to offset the added risk to the lender. Therefore, the leverage position of the subsidiary generally should not rise above some point (depending on the policy of the United States parent). But even in the event of high business risk (for example, recession), the subsidiary with a fairly high financial risk need not necessarily worry about the interest due to its lender if that lender is its parent because the parent can simply consider the unpaid interest of the subsidiary as an additional investment.

United States parent companies not only seem to prefer this form of financing for their subsidiaries, but they also seem to prefer debt to equity forms of financing. This is true for many reasons. The interest paid to the United States parent is tax deductible while dividend payments are not. Foreign governments tend to place stricter limits on the remittances of dividends than they do on interest payments to the United States parents. And, finally, foreign political risks encourage the parent to use debt to finance foreign subsidiaries. Subsidiaries therefore tend to prefer the practice of using above-average amounts of financing from their United States parents.

Research conducted by Cherukuri Rao and Robert Litzenberger compared firms in India to firms in the United States. They concluded that even though the Modigliani-Miller view tends to hold in a developed economy, the traditional view tends to hold in a less-developed economy. This very interesting conclusion, however, has been challenged by others and no definitive evaluation and conclusion has been achieved.[2]

There is certainly room for more empirical evidence and clarification of assumptions in both theories of optimal capital structure—espe-

---

[1]Robert Leftwich, "U.S. Multinational Companies: Profitability, Financial Leverage and Effective Income Tax Rates," *Survey of Current Business*, May 1974, p. 27.

[2]Cherukuri Rao and Robert Litzenberger, "Leverage and the Cost of Capital in a Less-Developed Capital Market: Comment," *Journal of Finance*, June 1971, pp. 777–82; and L. Sarma and Hanumanta Rao, "Reply," *ibid.*, pp. 783–85.

cially as to how they pertain to international business. At the present time, however, many American firms behave as if they were fact. As Stonehill and Stitzel point out, the publishers of industry ratios affect the decisions of institutional lenders, even though these ratios are usually just derived from one environment (namely, the United States).[3] A United States multinational corporation, of one industry, usually needs a different ratio to work with in each environment or nation in which it is operating a subsidiary. The subsidiary may need to borrow funds locally but, as a United States multinational, it may be forced to still perform according to the United States domestic industry financial structure norms. (This is especially true when the United States parent uses a consolidated balance sheet.)

Table 8-1 is included to illustrate just how different the leverage practices and norms are in various environments. It should be noted that debt-to-equity ratios in the United States industries are always among the lowest in the world. Japan, West Germany, and Sweden have relatively high financial ratios.

The financial structure norms for the industries in each nation are affected by several environmental factors. Stonehill and Stitzel point out that one of the main environmental factors affecting the financial structure norms in the nations in table 8-1 is the fact that the governments are usually unable to absorb major security floatations. The existing institutions (as a result of increased governmental dependency on these banks) are able to be both lender and stockholder of the corporations they support. This tends to reduce the lending institution's perceived risk of default on loans and, therefore, results in more loans and in higher debt financial structure norms.[4] Another environmental factor that affects the debt ratio norms is a nation's tax policy. These and many other factors, which vary from nation to nation, account for the numerous financial structure norms that the United States multinational corporations face.

Historically, the United States capital market was the main source of capital for the United States multinational and its subsidiaries. MNCs had to conform to United States industry financial structure norms in order to acquire capital from the United States capital market. As MNCs grew and developed, they often began acquiring capital abroad. As has been pointed out, overseas capital markets usually tolerate higher leverage ratios, but United States subsidiaries in these foreign environments were restricted by their parent company managers on the amount of debt they could acquire locally because of the accounting practice of using consolidated balance sheets. In fact,

---

[3]Arthur Stonehill and Thomas Stitzel, "Financial Structure and Multinational Corporations," *California Management Review*, Fall 1969, pp. 91–96.

[4]Ibid.

TABLE 8-1 Debt-to-Equity Ratios of Various Countries by Selected Industries

	Alcoholic Beverages	*Automobiles*	*Chemicals*	*Electrical*	*Foods*	*Iron & Steel*	*Nonferrous Metals*	*Paper*	*Textiles*	*Total*
Benelux	45.7	—	44.6	37.5	56.2	50.0	59.2	35.9	54.2	47.9
France	35.8	36.0	34.3	59.1	24.7	33.7	55.0	35.5	20.9	37.2
West Germany	59.2	55.1	54.8	64.5	42.5	63.8	68.1	71.8	44.9	58.6
Italy	64.9	77.3	68.2	73.6	68.4	77.9	67.5	—	66.6	70.3
Japan	60.9	70.3	73.2	71.1	78.3	74.5	74.5	77.7	76.6	72.5
Sweden	—	76.4	45.6	60.1	46.8	70.0	68.7	60.7	—	61.2
Switzerland	—	—	59.7	50.8	29.2	—	26.3	—	—	41.5
U.K.	43.8	56.5	38.7	46.9	47.6	44.9	41.7	46.6	42.4	45.5
U.S.	31.1	39.2	43.3	50.3	34.2	35.8	36.7	38.9	44.6	38.7
Total	48.8	58.7	51.4	57.4	47.3	56.3	55.3	51.7	49.4	—

SOURCE: Arthur Stonehill and Thomas Stitzel. "Financial Structure and Multinational Corporations," *California Management Review*, Fall 1969, p. 92.

often the MNCs still have to perform according to the United States norms even though such a policy may handicap the subsidiaries.

Conclusions

Stonehill and Stitzel suggest that, because of differing environmental factors, the subsidiaries ought to, wherever possible, adopt a financial structure similar to the industry norms and local cash flow patterns in the host country.[5] One of the significant results of such a practice would be a more efficient allocation of resources. (In economies where the interest rate is high, for example, a subsidiary would think twice before acquiring more capital than it can economically afford; that is, the rate of return on assets should exceed the local rate of interest.) Another result would be to enable subsidiaries to compare their own returns on equity with those of local foreign firms in that industry.

If subsidiaries localize their capital structures, then the consolidated balance sheet of the MNC will tend to show a debt ratio that is not in tune, in terms of United States dollars, with the norms of United States industry. But this should not be the only factor when considering the localization process. The firm should be analyzed from the firm's point of view rather than from external and often irrelevant viewpoints and criteria.

The use of irrelevant external standards often comes about because of the frequently accepted theoretical position that an optimal capital structure exists. As stated earlier, most domestic industries behave as if there were such an optimal financial structure for firms in each industry. But these norms evolved domestically under the effects of the variables in one environment. Multinational corporations must have a broader outlook. They need to consider all relevant foreign environmental variables if they intend to achieve anything close to optimal performance.

[5]Ibid.

Bibliography

Business International. "Determining A Corporatewide Debt/Equity Policy," *Management Monograph #57*, Business International Corporation, New York City, 1972.

Leftwich, Robert. "U.S. Multinational Companies: Profitability, Financial Leverage, and Effective Tax Rates." *Survey of Current Business*, May 1974, p. 27.

Rao, Cherukuri, and Robert Litzenberger, "Leverage and the Cost of Capital in a Less-Developed Capital Market: Comment." *Journal of Finance*, June 1971, pp. 777–82.

Remmers, Lee, Arthur Stonehill, Richard Wright, and Theo Beekhuisen, "Industry and Size as Debt Ratio Determinants in Manufacturing Internationally." *Financial Management*, Summer 1974, pp. 24–32.

Sarma, L., and Hanumanta Rao, "Leverage and the Cost of Capital in a Less-Developed Capital Market." *Journal of Finance*, September 1969, pp. 673–77.

———. "Leverage and the Cost of Capital in a Less-Developed Capital Market: Reply." *Journal of Finance*, June 1971, pp. 783–85.

Solnik, Bruno. "The International Pricing of Risk: An Empirical Investigation of the World Capital Market Structures." *Journal of Finance*, May 1974b, pp. 365–78.

Stonehill, Arthur, and Thomas Stitzel, "Financial Structure and Multinational Corporations." *California Management Review*, Fall 1969, pp. 91–96.

Toy, Norman, Arthur Stonehill, Lee Remmers, Richard Wright, and Theo. Beekhuisen, "A Comparative International Study of Growth, Profitability and Risk Determinants of Corporate Debt Ratios in the Manufacturing Sector." *Journal of Financial and Quantitative Analysis*, November 1974, pp. 875–886.

Short-Term Financing

BOTH domestic and international firms require short-term financing to meet working capital needs, for seasonal or temporary fluctuations, and for times when longer-term capital is not yet available. There are, however, major differences between domestic and international money market operations.

The biggest difference is that the variety of capital sources available internationally is far greater. Naturally, the larger variety requires a broader range of knowledge and a more sophisticated approach in decision making. The foreign exchange risks, for example, must be faced, but the problems and complexities are not extremely great. Multinational firms certainly feel that the risks and efforts are worthwhile—they are heavy users of the international money markets.

Classifying all the international sources for short-term funds is somewhat arbitrary because of the overlapping roles of the primary sources. Several sources, in fact, may be involved at any one time. However, this chapter will focus on the most important and widely used sources of short-term funds and methods of financing available to multinationals. These sources will be classified as follows:

1. Trade credit
2. Financial institutions
3. Eurocurrency market
4. Intracompany financing

Trade Credit

For a variety of reasons, trade credit is more complex internationally than in domestic business. Because international trade directly affects a country's balance of payments and the value of its currency, most governments pay a great deal of attention to all aspects of international trade. Although local businessmen may feel that the government requires too much red tape, the documents required domestically are nothing compared to what many governments require in international trade. Often the firm doing business overseas must seek the services of intermediaries such as banks to help them in preparing the necessary documents.

The fact that there are different currencies involved in international trade also adds complexity. At least one party must accept a contract expressed in a currency that is not his own. In order to reduce exchange rate risks, he may need to enter into other contracts and the extra steps and documents involved in doing so can be tricky.

Furthermore, in international trade the buyer and seller are often less familiar with each other than in domestic business. Distance and a general unavailability of international credit data make transactions more uncertain. Intermediaries are available to help ease this problem area and, once again, documents are involved in the use of their services.

It is this set of problems and the intermediaries and documents involved in dealing with them to which we now turn.

Export-Import Financing

A firm's international business involvement usually begins with an export or import idea. Various products or projects may be considered and their costs analyzed. If the prospects look good, negotiations between the buyer and seller must begin. Both parties must agree to price, quantity, type of currency, and payment and shipping terms. When the parties involved sign the contracts, the documents can be used in trade credit negotiations.

There are two types of international trade credit: credit may be arranged on an open account basis or it may be on the foreign collections basis. The *open account* basis is easier to arrange. The exporter sends the agreed-upon merchandise and accompanying documents to the importer. The importer pays when the items arrive. This method, of course, requires a level of trust usually possible only after the parties involved have had previously good business relations with one another.

The *foreign collections* basis differs from the open account in that a bank is used as an agent. Bank loans are not involved, but the bank does help prepare the documents and aids in transmitting payments. When the bank is also used as a supplier of credit, then letters of credit are normally used for international trade. The bank is no longer simply an agent, but is a third party in the negotiations and transactions. When the bank actually guarantees payment, trade credit in its pure form doesn't really exist.

Trade Documents

Even when traders do not use credit they are often required to use certain documents as specified by local regulations and international trade laws. There are two basic types of foreign trade documents: negotiable money paper and commodity paper. Money paper requires financial payment while commodity paper requires a payment in goods and services. Each type of paper will be discussed in turn.

There are several kinds of negotiable money paper currently being used. The promissory note and various forms of a "draft" note are the two most frequently used. The *promissory note* states a promise to pay a fixed amount at a specified time to the exporter. It is especially popular with businessmen involved in long-term projects because it reduces the paper work if there are several subsequent shippings. Terms are set at the start. When each shipment is made, the same terms can apply.

The *draft,* often also called a "bill of exchange," is used more frequently than the promissory note. It differs from a promissory note in that a third party—such as a bank—can be named as the recipient of the funds. Such a note permits the exporter to borrow the amount he will receive for the sale. He simply uses the draft as a form of collateral on the loan since the bank can be named as the recipient. (The exporter must still bear all liabilities unless other actions are taken.)

There are several types of drafts. "Clean drafts" are processed by the traders and are, in effect, foreign accounts receivable on an open account basis. Other types require bank assistance. The "sight draft" requires immediate payment upon delivery of the goods. "Acceptance drafts" allow a period of time before the payment is due. The importer simply signs his name, date, and the word "accepted" on the draft when it arrives. "Bankers' drafts" and bank money orders are additional forms of negotiable money paper which may be used in trade.

Commodity paper is less important than financial paper, but provides a function desired by many importers. Two types of commodity paper are the *bill of lading,* which is a carrier document, and the *warehouse receipt,* which is a storage document. Both are negotiable.

Since both financial and commodity paper can be used as negotiable instruments, they add flexibility in international business. These documents are considered as proof of ownership and can often be sold or used as collateral for short-term bank loans. If the documents are sold, they are usually sold at a discount in much the same way as domestic accounts receivable are sold to factoring companies.

Commercial Banks

As noted in the previous section, commercial banks are a major financial intermediary in trade credit. But banks also provide many other services and types of funds. In fact, the banks are the single most important external source of international short-term financing. The specific types of funds and services vary from country to country, but all countries have some funds available at local banks.

Most MNCs use more than one bank. Some even use more than one bank per country, but all their banking activities are usually coordinated through a large bank in the home country. Although the banking network might at first seem complex, it need not be since many banking practices are similar in most countries and many of the financial documents are almost internationally standardized.

Banks provide the typical lines of credit and regular commercial loans. They use drafts and are involved in trade credit as previously discussed. Overdrafts (writing checks beyond deposits) are often also permitted internationally—in fact, they are one of the major forms of short-term credit in Europe.

There are some banking practices which differ overseas, of course. Most banks overseas provide a broader range of functions than is permitted in the United States. They lend more longer-term money and are involved in investment banking. More financing is unsecured and trade notes and bills are more often discounted overseas. Discounting costs vary from country to country, but most developed countries have efficient means of handling the entire process.

Special Practices

Risks due to possible changes in currency values do force firms to seek special bank arrangements. Currency swaps and link financing are two types of arrangements which are often considered.

Currency swaps are mutual agreements made between parties to trade currencies for a fixed period of time and then trade the currencies back. The best known variation of such swaps is known as an "arbi loan." An arbi loan is arranged in a country where money is easily available at desirable rates. It is converted to the currency needed by the firm, but a contract is made to buy back the currency at a specified time in the future for a specified amount of the currency being used. (This is a "forward contract.") Currency swaps and arbi loans permit a firm to borrow in one market for use in another market with a definite knowledge as to what it will pay for the loan. No exchange risks exist.

The cost for such arrangements is the interest rate plus exchange expenses. If the forward currency contract involves a price much different than current (spot) exchange rates, then the real expense can be quite high. It is up to the financial manager to determine if the exchange risks are great enough that a premium should be paid to remove them.

Link financing is used in countries where the currencies are so weak that there may not be an acknowledged exchange rate or forward market. Banks in strong-currency countries aid firms in weak-currency countries by guaranteeing repayment on the loans that these firms need. The firm either borrows from a local bank or a local firm with excess "weak" money. Of course, the bank in the strong currency country usually wants some sort of deposit from the firm's parent company and the local firm must pay local interest rates.

All these new options, terms, documents, and methods may scare off potential international businessmen, but they should not. Banks are quite willing to take care of all the paper work related to credit, billing, and collection of payments for international trade. No firm should be intimidated by the slightly different documents necessary. Most large banks have experienced staffs and charge very little for their expertise.

The Eurocurrency Market

It must be noted, though, that the international money market has more than just new credit instruments and expanded banking services. New types of money are also available. Each country has a currency which it controls, but most developed countries also have currencies which they do not control. These are called "Eurocurrencies."

Eurocurrencies are money deposited outside the control of the country of origin—usually in foreign banks. Dollars deposited in France or Italy, for example, are called "Eurodollars." British pounds deposited in Italy or the United States are called "Eurosterling" or "Europounds."

The Eurocurrency market is very well organized, very efficient, and very large. One reason for its existence is the almost total absence of international controls. But another reason for its popularity is the ready availability of its money—often at lower interest rates than those prevailing elsewhere. Rates can be low because controls (especially reserve requirements) are often zero. Naturally, from the point of view of businessmen, such currencies are desirable. Governments want more controls, but agree that Eurocurrencies provide a very important function in international business. Economists worry that a credit failure may set up a chain reaction in the long link of Eurocurrency loans frequently involved, but few recommend that Eurocurrencies be done away with.

Since there are few controls and many who borrow and lend in any one Eurocurrency, the exact size of the market is unknown. However, most estimate the market at over $60 billion. Loans are not small either—averaging about $5 million.

Supply and demand conditions determine prevailing interest rates. The rates and terms are published daily in many of the world's leading financial papers. Whenever a businessman is interested in considering such a loan, all he need do is call his bank.

Other names for portions of the Eurocurrency market have been recently used. It is now possible to refer to "Asian currencies" or "Asian dollars" to identify those in Asia. There are also references to "Petrodollars." Such names refer to obvious classes of money outside the country of origin, but it should be remembered that all such groupings are but subsets of the vast money market known as the "Eurocurrency" market.

Summary

This chapter has identified the important instruments involved in international trade credit. It has discussed the various roles and practices of banks when working with MNCs. Additionally, a new type of money was described—Eurocurrency.

MNCs use trade credit, banks, and the Eurocurrency market, but these are not their only sources of short-term money. In fact, most firms first check the cash available at headquarters and at the various subsidiaries of the MNC around the world to first determine if sufficient funds are available within the total corporation. Since intracompany funds are so often available and since they are so important in short-term financing, they are the subject of the next chapter.

Bibliography

Business International Corporation. *Financing Foreign Operations.* Current issues.

Carson, Deane. "Government Policies and the Eurodollar Market." *Columbia Journal of World Business* 10 (no. 4, 1975): 58–64.

Clendenning, E. Wayne. "Euro-Dollars: The Problem of Control." *The Banker,* April 1968, pp. 321–29.

Davis, Steven. "A Buyer's Market in Eurodollars." *Harvard Business Review,* May 1973, pp. 119–30.

———. "U.S. Banks Abroad: One-Stop Shopping?" *Harvard Business Review,* July-August 1971, pp. 75–84.

Dufey, Gunter. "Innovations in International Money and Capital Markets." *Michigan Business Review,* May 1970, pp. 19–24.

Einzig, Paul. *Parallel Money Markets.* London: Macmillan and Co., Ltd., 1971.

———. *The Eurodollar System.* New York: St. Martin's Press, Inc., 1966.

Eiteman, David, and Arthur Stonehill, *Multinational Business Finance.* Reading, Mass.: Addison-Wesley Publishing Company, Inc., 1973. pp. 82–144.

Klopstock, Fred. *The Euro-Dollar Market: Some Unresolved Issues.* Princeton, N.J.: International Finance Section, Princeton University, 1968.

Lewis, Furman, and W. R. Hoskins, "The Eurodollar Markets." *Business Horizons,* April 1970, pp. 49–60.

Madden, John, and Marcus Nadler, *The International Money Markets.* Englewood Cliffs, N.J.: Prentice-Hall, Inc., 1968.

Nehrt, Lee. *International Finance for Multinational Business,* 2nd ed. Scranton, Pa.: Intext, Inc., 1972. pp. 400–64.

Prindl, R. Andreas. "Guidelines for MNC Money Managers." *Harvard Business Review,* January-February 1976, pp. 73–80.

Robbins, Sidney, and Robert Stobaugh, *Money in the Multinational Enterprise.* New York: Basic Books, Inc., 1973.

Swoboda, Alexander. *The Euro-Dollar Market: An Interpretation.* Princeton, N.J.: International Finance Section, Princeton University, 1968.

Von Clemm, Michael. "The Rise of Consortium Banking." *Harvard Business Review,* May-June 1971, pp. 125–42.

Weston, J. Fred, and Bart Sorge, *International Managerial Finance.* Homewood, Ill.: Richard D. Irwin, Inc., 1972. pp. 161–207.

Zenoff, David, and Jack Zwick, *International Financial Management,* Prentice-Hall, Inc., 1969. pp. 275–411.

Zinn, Eberhard. "The International Money and Capital Market of the Euro-Currencies." *European Business,* April 1969, pp. 59–65.

```
101010101010101010101010101010101010101010101010101010101010101010101010101010101010
101010101010101010101010101010101010101010101010101010101010101010101010101010101010
1010101010101010101010101010101010101   10101   101010101010101010101010101010101010
10101010101010101010101010101010101010   010   0101010101010101010101010101010101010
101010101010101010101010101010101010101   1   10101010101010101010101010101010101010
1010101010101010101010101010101010101010     010101010101010101010101010101010101010
10101010101010101010101010101010101010101   1010101010101010101010101010101010101010
1010101010101010101010101010101010101010     010101010101010101010101010101010101010
101010101010101010101010101010101010101   1   10101010101010101010101010101010101010
10101010101010101010101010101010101010   010   0101010101010101010101010101010101010
1010101010101010101010101010101010101   10101   101010101010101010101010101010101010
101010101010101010101010101010101010101010101010101010101010101010101010101010101010
101010101010101010101010101010101010101010101010101010101010101010101010101010101010
```

Parent-Subsidiary Financing

Flows of money between a parent firm and its subsidiaries are nothing new. Although not the most important single source of funds, intracompany cash movements were common long before there were multinational corporations. Such money movements are still fairly common in international business but they are now made under far more complicated conditions.

Most company policies endeavor to have the subsidiaries finance themselves as much as possible from local sources—unless the cost of doing so would be excessive. But, regardless of what headquarters would prefer, there are frequent occasions when local sources of finance are either insufficient, inappropriate, or simply unavailable to meet the subsidiary's needs. In such circumstances, the parent company has to provide supplemental or substitute financing or risk endangering the future success of its investment.

While this might at first be viewed as a parent firm's liability, it should be noted that these situations are actually excellent opportunities for MNCs. The subsidiary's competition is probably also encountering the same problems which are due to a local money shortage. If the competition does not have comparable international connections, then it may be unable to secure necessary funds. The subsidiary, therefore, may have a competitive advantage by obtaining funds from its parent company.

However, advantages in intracompany financing are not without added problems for MNCs. Governmental regulations, different rates of inflation, differing interest rates, and risks of currency changes all force more careful evaluation of requests for international fund transfers. All of these added risks and problems must be considered, but they vary among countries over time depending upon the type of funding requested.

Alternative Financing Methods

While numerous mechanisms exist for transferring funds within the MNC network, basically only three are used by parent firms to supply their foreign affiliates. These three methods are loans (both formal and informal), equity financing, and parent-subsidiary trade credit.

Loans from the Parent Organization

From the evidence that is available, it appears that loans from parent organizations represent the largest single source of funds supplied from within the corporate network.[1] These loans are usually made on a formal basis, though in some instances informal advances have been used. Formal loans, as their name implies, have a fixed rate of interest and a set payment schedule. In contrast, informal loans or advances are made with unspecified interest rates and no fixed due date. Even though this latter method offers advantages in terms of flexibility, the passage of the Revenue Act of 1962 has made its use obsolete by specifying that a "reasonable" repayment schedule must be specified in advance on any loans made if the parent is to avoid having repayments taxed as income earned. As a consequence, most loans made to subsidiaries since 1962 have been made on a formal basis.

Even though most loans are made on a formal basis, they do offer certain advantages that other forms of parent-subsidiary funding do not. In most instances, the repayment of loans by the subsidiary can often reduce taxes in the host country as well as in the United States. As of 1968, for instance, European and Canadian governments, like the United States, permit companies incorporated within their borders to deduct interest expenses from taxable income. In addition, repayment of principal is not included as income for the parent organization.

In countries where repayment of interest on loans does not reduce the impact of taxes, loans may still provide a method of withdrawing

[1]Michael Brooke and H. Lee Remmers, *The Strategy of Multinational Enterprise* (New York: American Elsevier Publishing Company, Inc., 1970).

earnings. In many less-developed countries, the payment of dividends to the parent organization can lead to charges of exploitation. The payment of interest, instead of earnings, can reduce the associated political and social criticism. In addition, some less-developed countries (such as India and Brazil) restrict the amount of earnings that can be remitted to the parent organization. Interest payments offer a viable alternative.

Finally, and probably most importantly, loans offer the greatest flexibility in terms of moving funds within the corporate network. This means that a loan made to one subsidiary can be transferred to a sister subsidiary if the need arises when the former subsidiary no longer needs the funds. This type of transfer can also be used to reduce the risk of foreign exchange loss or the impact of taxation.

Equity Financing

While there are many advantages associated with meeting subsidiaries' financial needs through loans from the parent organization, equity financing does offer an alternative. This method of parent-subsidiary funding is most typically done with issued capital (i.e., the transfer of cash for common stock). In recent years, however, especially in less-developed countries, contributions of technology, patents, trademarks, machinery, etc., have been used in lieu of cash. After the initial investment to establish a subsidiary, however, very little equity capital is usually issued. In fact, most firms operating abroad find it advantageous to minimize the amount of issued capital. In some countries, however, earnings which exceed a certain proportion of issued capital are taxed at a more severe rate. Firms with operations in these countries, therefore, may find issued capital an attractive way to meet their subsidiaries' financing needs.

Issued capital is not the only method available to increase the equity base of a subsidiary. By altering the proportion of earnings remitted, the parent company can increase the net worth of its subsidiary. Of course it would require a significant number of years to make substantial changes. A firm cannot simply make radical changes in retained earnings without receiving unwanted attention from local tax authorities. As a result, virtually all firms attempt to maintain dividends at a relatively constant rate.

Parent-Subsidiary Trade Credit

The third mechanism which can be used to transfer funds from the parent organization to its subsidiaries involves the use of trade credit. By extending the length of the payment period for inventory supplied by the parent organization, the parent corporation is, in effect, supplying funds to its subsidiaries. (The subsidiary sells the inventory and uses the revenue for a while before repaying the parent.) This type of subsidiary financing is used most frequently, though not exclusively, by manufacturing industries who supply their subsidiaries with high-priced intermediate goods that are assembled or manufactured abroad, and by multinational firms with sales organizations abroad.

When used as a means of financing a subsidiary's operations, trade credit is most frequently extended on an open account basis. This form provides for the greatest flexibility. In many circumstances, this method has even replaced the informal loan since it offers the same advantages in terms of responsiveness to the subsidiary's needs.

Which Method is Best?

Several factors determine whether the parent company will provide funds as equity or as an intracompany loan (in cash or in trade credit). The major factors include local regulations and customs, the length of time the funds will be needed, the amount of funds that will be needed, tax considerations, attitudes toward risk, and other intangibles. Perhaps most important is the amount of flexibility the company feels it must have to shift funds between various organizations in the group. Although this concern with flexibility is primarily dependent upon tax considerations and attitudes toward risk, it is also a reflection of the degree of financial sophistication that has been reached in the effort to manage a common pool of corporate funds.

The first factor to consider when determining whether to supply equity or an intracompany loan is the local regulations. For initial start-up costs, at least a minimum of equity from the parent company will have to be supplied. Many countries have specific laws stating even the amount of equity required. But even in other countries, local banks may require a certain minimum ratio of equity to total capital before loans are available. If a company wishes to keep its equity contributions to a minimum, banks will probably require intracompany loans to be subordinated to the local debt. In some countries, tax or exchange control regulations provide special incentives for firms using additional equity. India and New Zealand, for example, have higher taxes on profits that exceed a certain proportion of equity. Other countries limit dividend payments to some ratio of issued capital.

Second, the degree of permanence of the need for funds is an important determinant of whether equity or intracompany loans are used. Where the need is felt to be temporary, companies frequently prefer to use an intracompany loan. If, as sometimes happens, the funds prove to be needed for a very long time, the subsidiary can always capitalize them at any time. What companies consider to be a long time varies a great deal. Where a relatively rapid pay-back schedule is projected and especially where the subsidiary is expected to be able to finance a substantial part of its needs from local sources, it seems reasonable for a parent company to consider very little of its investment as a permanent commitment. In such cases, it makes good sense to have as much as possible of the supplied funds in the form of intracompany loans even though the temporary result is that the subsidiary is undercapitalized.

Companies that are relatively inexperienced in foreign operations tend to prefer intracompany loans and undercapitalization of foreign subsidiaries. Capital invested in the form of intracompany debt is subject to many of the same sort of risks as an equity contribution, but the inexperienced parent company believes that it can obtain a higher cash flow return by repatriating loans rather than through dividends. Therefore, the loan is viewed as a more retrievable commitment than an equity contribution. Another reason these firms tend to favor loans is that the ready availability of equity contributions from the parent may not be conducive for locally effective financial management. The need to meet required loan repayments may be a useful incentive for inexperienced subsidiary managers.

Experienced foreign investors, however, point out that undercapitalization limits the subsidiary's ability to obtain local funds so they strive for a well-balanced capital structure for their subsidiaries. Foreign lenders are reluctant to extend long-term credit to American-owned subsidiaries whose debt to equity ratio is unsually high. Furthermore, local governments sometimes strenuously object to a debt element that is too high. This is especially true in countries having balance-of-payment problems when it appears to the local authorities that dividend payments to the parent company are being supported by local borrowing.

Host governments sometimes examine more than just the debt to equity ratio. They may inquire into the relationship of earned surplus to capital account. Some companies may be subjected, because of this, to pressure by local governments to transfer funds from the subsidiary's surplus account into its capital account. Since funds held in an earned surplus account can be declared as an accumulated dividend and thus repatriated, it is understandable that a foreign government should be concerned with the effects that such repatriation may have on its national balance of payments.

Inexperienced investors are not the only ones to favor the use of loans instead of equity contributions. Most foreign investors have indicated that loans are the preferred financing of subsidiaries in economically unstable areas. Brazil and other Latin American countries are illustrations of countries where, in recent years, repatriation of earnings as dividends has been virtually impossible, while arrangements for loan repayments have been fully honored. In less risky countries, though, the decision as to debt or equity funding for the subsidiary is much more likely to hinge on the more standard economic factors—which will give the firm the greatest flexibility in maximizing future flows of funds to the parent.[2]

It should be noted that one of the main advantages of using intracompany debt rather than equity is that it can often reduce taxes. Such repayments are generally allowed without penalty. But if the subsidiary is financed with equity, then repayment is possible only with after-tax earnings. Furthermore, these repayments are usually subject to an additional tax when received by the parent company. The result can be that the subsidiary may need to make substantially more money to repay equity than to repay debt.

Loans to subsidiaries also enable the parent firm to charge a premium—an interest. This may have two advantages. First of all, as noted earlier, there is the probability of a tax advantage since interest payments are considered costs and, therefore, lower the reported earnings subject to taxes. There is also the possibility that the ongoing subsidiary will generate fewer political problems by paying interest rather than dividends. Countries generally prefer more (rather than less) equity originally, but, in later years, may point to dividend payments as "proof" of profiteering or exploitation.

Flexibility is another major advantage achieved when financing with loans. The subsidiary may repay its debts whenever funds are available. In fact, they may not even need to send the money to the parent. Rather, they may simply shift funds between the subsidiary and other organizations within the corporation. This is especially easy if the MNC has established a financial network to "pool" its resources. Such a "pooling" of resources, in fact, can reduce the needs of each subsidiary in the organization.

Intracompany loans can also help to reduce exchange loss. It is probably impossible to avoid some losses due to currency changes, but the proper timing of money investments would greatly help reduce the risks. The trick, of course, is in the timing. However, debt provides a better vehicle for moving funds exposed to currency problems than does equity financing.

Changing the credit terms on intracompany trade is another way to reduce losses due to currency changes. The strategy is to charge subsidiaries sooner when the currency is weakening. If the currency is strong, longer credit terms to the subsidiary are possible. The subsid-

[2]For a more complete description of corporate practices, see the publication by Judd Polk, Irene Meister, and Lawrence Veit, *U.S. Production Abroad and the Balance of Payments* (New York: The National Industrial Conference Board, 1966).

iary itself can change its own credit terms to the parent or fellow subsidiaries depending upon currency forecasts. Changes in the interest rate are not as easily accepted by tax authorities. The price of goods is more visible and more controlled than the length of time credit is extended (if it is extended at all).

Local vs. Parent Financing

The typical subsidiary usually obtains funds from local sources. This is the way most parent firms want it and there are many good reasons for this. Local funds are not subject to losses due to local currency devaluations, the local financial community is happy when borrowing is done locally (although other businesses seeking funds may not be so happy because it uses up the money available and drives up local borrowing costs), debt repayment is easy since there are no exchange expenses or restrictions, the repayment is more politically acceptable locally since it does not create a financial drain from the community or hurt the host country's balance of payments (but, of course, the initial borrowing did not help either), and local borrowing seems to act as an aid to subsidiary managers in that it forces them to fully recognize their financial costs and responsibilities. Some MNCs feel that money from headquarters is not as fully "respected." Tax considerations may also make local borrowing more attractive.

On the other side of the coin, there are times and situations when it is better to obtain money from the parent. Costs are usually higher abroad. When the higher costs are due primarily to higher inflation rates, then currency devaluations are likely and local borrowing is probably worth the extra costs since it reduces these currency risks. However, when higher borrowing costs are due primarily to a shortage of available capital, then it is usually better to obtain funds elsewhere. Naturally, if no local money is available at all—a condition which often exists for long-term funds in less-developed countries—then there is no decision to make. Generally, the longer the time that funds are needed, the poorer the country, the newer the subsidiary to the local business community, and the smaller the MNC, the harder it is to borrow locally.

Bibliography

Brooke, Michael, and H. Lee Remmers, *The Strategy of Multinational Enterprise*. New York: American Elsevier Publishing Company, Inc., 1970.

Eiteman, David, and Arthur Stonehill, *Multinational Business Finance*. Reading, Mass.: Addison-Wesley Publishing Company, Inc., 1973. pp. 69–81.

Greene, James, and Michael Duerr, *Intercompany Transactions in the Multinational Firm*. New York: The National Industrial Conference Board, 1970.

Polk, Judd, Irene Meister, and Lawrence Veit, *U.S. Production Abroad and the Balance of Payments*. New York: The National Industrial Conference Board, 1966.

Stobaugh, Robert, Jr. "Financing Foreign Subsidiaries of U.S. Controlled Multinational Enterprises." *Journal of International Business Studies*, Summer 1970, pp. 43–64.

Long-Term Financing

MULTINATIONAL corporations have many financing options open to them. They may use internal funds, they may obtain their capital from sources within their home country, or they may seek funds abroad. Domestic firms, of course, have these same options, but seldom consider foreign sources. For the MNCs, however, access to foreign markets—especially the bond markets—is important. This chapter will examine the types of long-term financing available, the risks of using each source, restrictions frequently encountered, and the roles of investment bankers and other intermediaries.

Sources

Multinational corporation subsidiaries can issue stock or bonds in most of the local markets of the countries in which they operate. There are a few countries which prohibit this, but a more frequent problem is that many countries simply do not have large enough capital markets to meet the subsidiary's needs. The number of such countries is declining, however, and many countries are actively encouraging MNCs to enter their markets.

Just as in other areas of corporate finance, long-term financing involves many differences overseas. Take the concept of stock certificates, for example. While most shares in the United States are registered, most shares in Europe are bearer shares. The issuing firm has no list of stockholders and must wait for dividend payment requests in order to pay declared dividends.

Preferred stock is issued, but it is less popular abroad. One reason why this is so is that such shares are intended to give a more special treatment to one class of stockholders (generally insiders) than the other investors are generally willing to tolerate.

Practices also differ as to voting power. Some shares have added power because voting is weighted according to length of time the stock has been owned. In these countries, it is harder to attract interest in new shares.

The average sale is often larger in Europe because a larger proportion of issues are purchased by financial institutions. In fact, most European banks are permitted to purchase stock for their own portfolios (an act not allowed in the United States).

In many countries, short selling is prohibited. Although this does not directly affect the MNC, it tends to reduce investor interest in equity markets and limits the volume of transactions. Fewer daily transactions may also result in a less stable market.

There are also differences in the way stock prices are quoted. They can be listed in monetary units or as a percentage of some nominal value. Each market has its own method, requirements for listing firms, and charges for having a firm's stock listed. These charges can be substantial. In fact, most MNCs find that it is too expensive to list their stock in every market. What they usually do is to list only in those countries where they have the heaviest level of business commitments.

A final difference that needs to be mentioned here is the practice abroad of paying out a higher percentage of earnings in dividends. Dividend yield reports are more important abroad because most overseas investors seem to prefer the dividend to capital gains. The United States firm issuing stock abroad should carefully consider this. Since many overseas firms only report enough earnings to pay the dividend the firm wants to declare, their payout ratio is very high. By comparison, the MNC might look bad. If it is to avoid a stock price decline, it should explain its reporting and dividend policy at the outset. Naturally, if the policy is to retain earnings, then the firm should be prepared for possible problems in issuing the shares. (Much more will be said about this in a subsequent discussion of profit remission and retained earnings policy in chapter 13.)

Multinational Issues

If, for some reason, the firm is not able to get funds in the host country, one option available to the subsidiary is to issue securities in a third country. Since the issue would probably be denominated in the currency of that country, this may result in the additional risk of currency changes in the country where the security was issued. If the third country has a strong currency, the dividends and repayments will be more expensive later. For this reason, choosing a country in which to obtain funds can be as important as deciding which type of funds to use or even what project the funds will be used for.

The capital markets that are open to MNCs do not have the breadth and depth of the United States market. This usually means that it is harder to raise large sums without paying higher costs. This higher cost is sometimes offset by a reduction of foreign exchange risks if the funds can be raised.

Instead of issuing securities in single national markets, another choice available to a firm is to issue Eurobonds or Euroequities. A general definition of a Eurobond is a bond, usually issued in Europe, by a firm outside its home country. It can be payable in a currency of a third country. United States firms, for example, have sold many bonds throughout western Europe which are payable in German marks. An issue can be placed in many different countries, but it usually is denominated in the currency of only one country. Thus, the geographical market range of a Eurobond is much wider than an issue on a single national exchange.

Eurobonds can be denominated in almost any currency or they can be in terms of a European Unit of Account (EUA). The EUA is an artificial currency composed of a formula of other currencies and referenced to gold (this will be discussed later). Most Eurobonds, however, are denominated in dollars and in strong currencies of Europe.

Eurobonds have many benefits compared to conventional bonds issued in single national (foreign) markets. Some governments place fewer restrictions on capital movements for Eurobonds. Disclosure requirements for many non–United States firms are often lower. The size of the issue can be larger so the unit costs of issuance can be lowered. Additionally, there is the advantage of added flexibility. A firm can simply choose the currency in which it wishes to make payments. (The choice, of course, will definitely affect the marketability of the issue.)

A recent development is the issuance of Euroequities. Euroequities are similar to Eurobonds, but are stock rather than bonds. The concept is too new to be fully evaluated yet, but appears to have added yet another option to the MNC seeking funds.

Development Banks

There are many financial institutions which lend money and capital to businesses. Some of these are unique to international business and are of special interest because of the services they provide. They are known as "development banks" and operate as nonprofit organizations for the sole purpose of aiding in economic development. They do this by making capital available at very favorable terms to the borrower.

The best-known development bank is the International Bank for Reconstruction and Development (IBRD)—better known as the "World Bank." This bank borrows and lends money around the world. It has two branches, the International Development Association (IDA) and the International Finance Corporation (IFC). Most of the loans from IDA are made in the poorer nations for major economic projects such as power plant or highway construction, agriculture development, or for a communication system such as a telephone exchange. The loans are on such favorable terms that IDA loses money. In order to help the World Bank break even, the IFC lends to the private sector on somewhat more realistic terms. It helps fund projects such as the construction of manufacturing plants. IFC terms are still very good and MNCs may apply (although some claim that local firms get priority).

There are many other development banks. Some are regional in scope while others are national. The best known regional bank is probably the Inter-American Development Bank (IDB). (It is known in Latin America as the Banco Interamericano Desarrollo.) Although it has had a few more political problems than the World Bank has had, it is widely known for its work in Latin America.

National banks have also played major roles in attracting and issuing capital for projects deemed an aid to development. Naturally, some of these banks have been more successful than others. Generally, the less favoritism given and the more strictly the loan is tied to expected economic contribution, the more successful the bank. In most cases, however, those receiving the loan have benefited (even if the country has not). Therefore, any firm considering a project which might be deemed "economically beneficial for the development of the country" should consider applying for a loan from the host country's development bank.

Risk

Some of the major differences between international and domestic financial managerial problems are the business, foreign exchange, and political risks that uniquely confront the multinational firm. The number of risks and their impact on long-term financing are far greater internationally than domestically. When a corporation seeks to raise funds across national borders, the major risks that it must evaluate and compensate for are exchange rate changes and controls. Both bonds and stocks are affected.

Greater perceived risks of foreign operations may increase the cost of equity. There are risks accompanying floatation. As the probability of fluctuation in price increases, the risks and costs may also increase.

There are also risks associated with dividends. The cost of converting dividends into the currency of the holder involves the risk of changes in the exchange rate or of changes in government restrictions on the conversion of its currency. Investors in strong-currency countries are not inclined to buy stock denominated in weak currencies unless the expected return fully compensates for these risks. Such criteria can be very expensive for the issuing firm.

Exchange Rate Risks

Bonds are also greatly affected by foreign exchange risk. For many multinational companies, the higher nominal cost usually encountered in borrowing abroad may be offset by a corresponding lowering of the foreign exchange risk. Replacing home-currency investment with local borrowing reduces the exposure to a foreign exchange devaluation.

It should be noted, however, that higher borrowing costs are not always a reflection of higher risks of currency changes (usually due to higher levels of inflation). The higher borrowing costs may be simply due to capital shortages. When the costs are high due to inflation, then the added costs are usually worth accepting in order to reduce the higher currency risks. But when these high costs are due primarily to capital shortages, then it is usually better for the subsidiary to seek funds in another country.

Reduction of foreign exchange risks is but one reason why firms are often willing to pay higher costs for overseas funds. Another reason is that borrowing locally may improve host country reception and reduce criticism. This is no sure thing, however, because capital movements work both ways. If the money is obtained locally, then repayments and interest or dividends do not hurt the balance of payments and do aid local investors, but the country experiences no capital inflow and other potential borrowers complain that the MNC drives up interest rates. On the other hand, if capital is brought in, then it will eventually come out at the expense of the host country's balance of payments.

During the sixties under the fixed exchange rate system, changes in the values of currencies of the less-developed nations of the world were common, but companies developed methods to protect themselves against large losses. Analyzing the possible ultimate costs of borrowing on the international capital markets in currencies other than that of the country where the parent company is domiciled is now an even more difficult task because the monetary system itself is complex with different countries adhering to different exchange rate systems. Many currencies in the world still remain fixed in terms of some reference currency. A number of currencies maintain fixed linkage with one another and do not move beyond agreed limits of fluctuation (for example, in the Common Market countries). There are also the independent floaters whose currencies supposedly move according to supply-and-demand forces in the market place and can fluctuate considerably on a day-to-day basis. Even these currencies are monitored to an extent.

Changes in currency values occur more frequently now, but in smaller amounts. New and increasingly complex instruments are being devised to adapt borrowing and lending to the evolving environment of unstable and floating exchange rates. There is a choice of currencies involved and investors may be residents of a country with a different currency. This can substantially influence the market, particularly when one of the currencies is weak or when there are exchange rate uncertainties creating risks for one or both parties. Weak currencies will always be in demand by borrowers because liabilities in these currencies will cost less if the currency depreciates. Strong currencies will be less in demand because the opposite is true.

When single-currency bonds are used, the risk is fully absorbed by the party dealing in the other party's currency. Some fear that there is a growing instability in the foreign exchange markets and that this may severely restrict the free flow of funds in international capital markets.[1] In order to reduce this risk, it may be necessary to spread the risk. One way to apportion this risk is by using mixed currency instruments in the Eurobond market.

There are two mixed-currency instruments. One is the European Unit of Account (EUA). The EUA is defined with reference to gold. All settlements are made in one of nine reference currencies (the nine European Common Market currencies). The conversion rate between a reference currency and the Unit of Account is based on currency parities that have been established by law or government decision. At the time of issue, the EUA is defined in the loan agreement with reference to all nine currencies. The individual values change and new conversion rates are instituted. However, individual parity changes do not alter the gold value of the EUA itself. When all reference currencies have changed their parities, then the gold value of the EUA can be modified. The borrower chooses the reference currency in which he wishes to receive the proceeds of the issue—usually the currency that trades at the highest premium in relation to its parity (since every fixed-parity currency is allowed to fluctuate within a limited range). Thus the EUA can lessen exchange risk or smooth the fluctuations of changing currency values.

The European Composite Unit (Eurco) is another composite currency method used to reduce potential foreign exchange losses of bond holders. The idea is to link the value of a bond to the European cur-

---

[1]Peter Lusztig and Bernhard Schwab, "Units of Accounting and the International Bond Market," *Columbia Journal of World Business*, Spring 1975, p. 75.

rency rates. Relative weighting is allotted to each of the Common Market currencies based on the economic significance of each country. Although the composition is fixed, the value of each component will vary slightly from day to day, with the Eurco reacting to each exchange rate change. As with the EUA, the borrower selects the currency in which purchases are to be made.

Mixed currency units show advantages beyond the spreading of exchange rate risk between borrower and lender. With units of account defined in the context of the Common Market, individual governments of member countries are less likely to interfere with restrictive legislation which may otherwise apply to foreign currency bonds. The larger market can also have a favorable impact on secondary trading.

Exchange Controls

There is a definite interrelationship between exchange controls, inflation, and devaluation. If the rate of inflation in a given country is greater than the rates of its main trading partners, the result will usually be a deficit in the balance of trade. This will often result in a deficit in the balance of payments. Consecutive deficits in the balance of payments cause a decrease in the foreign exchange reserves. A dangerously low level in foreign exchange reserves will force the government into instituting exchange controls and restrictions of one kind or another. (Exchange controls refer to governmental actions which limit the freedom of banks, companies, or individuals to buy and sell foreign exchange.) But these exchange controls do not solve the basic problem; they only postpone the inevitable devaluation.

A devaluation does not solve the basic problem either; it merely readjusts relative prices so that the country may, at least temporarily, achieve a balance or a surplus in its foreign trade. The basic problem is usually internal. Something is often causing an abnormally high rate of inflation. Until this problem is held in line, there will be more currency changes and exchange controls and other restrictions.

Restrictions

Most causes of inflation and currency devaluation are beyond the responsibility of MNCs. Nevertheless, governments often blame MNCs and seek to limit their actions. Not only must the multinational corporation observe the controls that are imposed domestically, but the company must also see to it that a whole host of international restrictions that arise in a particular country or region are met.

In order to fully understand governmental restrictions on capital movements, it is necessary to take a broader perspective. There are some fundamental reasons why governments find it necessary to take such actions.

The United States has a Securities and Exchange Commission to help protect the investor and provide an orderly market. Other countries have somewhat similar regulative agencies. Since the markets in smaller countries are more limited ("thinner"), however, their authorities often exercise more control. In addition to preventing fraud and aiding in providing for an orderly market, these authorities attempt to stabilize yields and often have the power (and responsibility) to give priority to the public sector over the private sector. In many countries, these authorities also give priority in their markets to domestic issuers over foreign issuers.

To the extent that these regulatory agencies aid their economies, they are filling a necessary role. After all, some MNCs are so large that a major sale of stock or issuance of bonds could soak up all available capital and radically alter the price of money. Since this is really in no one's best interest, some governmental controls and restrictions are necessary.

Unfortunately, not all restrictions have proven helpful. There have been many cases, especially in less-developed countries, where restrictions have only proved to limit economic development. The regulators in some countries even help manipulate the markets to their own advantages. These same "leaders" argue that no capital is available when it is often the case that their own people don't trust local offerings and will not invest. If a foreign firm is permitted to raise funds, it is embarrassing to watch how readily capital becomes available (it is actually "dug up" in many cases). Such is not always the case, though, because even in thin markets MNC securities can be manipulated when the regulators fail to fulfill their responsibilities.

Restrictions can take many forms. They may be absolute—no repayments at all—or they may be partial. Interest may be repaid, but not principal, for example. They may also be based on relative variables such as past performance. France, for example, would not allow dividends to be remitted that exceeded previous dividends by more than five percent.

In addition, some banking authorities practice limitations as to the term, date, and amount of issue. The Netherlands, Belgium, Luxembourg, and Italy practice these types of arrangements. Germany has had a restriction that any issue placed by a German firm outside Germany must keep twenty percent of the loaned amount above DM100,000 in Germany interest free. Reasons given for these restrictions are:

1. To eliminate temporary overloading of the market
2. To stabilize rates of yield
3. To assign the priority of public-sector needs over the private sector

Some countries will help in financing if the investment can be shown to be in the interest of the public sector. Ireland, for example, has financed eighty percent of certain plant construction. Britain, Belgium, France, and Italy have permitted bonds or equities to be issued more easily if the projects were to be in developing regions that are underutilized but have restricted issues elsewhere.

One problem is that governments have enacted laws which discourage foreign stock ownership. Britain, for example, placed a twenty percent surcharge on all purchases of nonsterling shares. Scandinavian countries have also restricted the ownership of capital stocks. But it must be noted that governmental restrictions are not the only reasons why people are not very interested in foreign equities. In many of the poorer countries, the vast majority of the population is too poor and the wealthy people have more lucrative opportunities. The threat of expropriation discourages some, but for others it is simply that there is not enough of a market or enough financial intermediaries to facilitate an orderly or dependable market.

Consideration must also be given to the useability of the different currencies in which bonds or equities are issued. Kuwait, for example, has started to issue bonds, but its currency is not the most readily tradeable yet. The United States dollar, the West German deutschmark, and the Swiss franc are still the most readily useable. Out of thirty-three companies issuing bonds between April and December 1973, fourteen issued in Swiss francs, eleven in dollars, five in deutschmarks, one in the European Unit of Account, one in French francs, and one in British pound sterling.[2]

The easiest places in which to obtain long-term funds are in the Eurobond and the Euroequity markets. They involve the fewest restrictions and can spread risk across several currencies. These instruments arose out of the Interest Equalization tax imposed by the United States that almost, in effect, closed down New York as a source of international capital funds. Some of the Eurobonds have "sweeteners" such as convertible features or warrants. The costs may be a bit higher in such issues, but they are easier to sell.

The results of tax on long-term borrowings have a profound restrictive effect on the issue. In a country where a tax is imposed on the interest a foreign lender receives, a thirty percent tax rate would reduce a nine percent yield down to 6.36 percent. Companies wishing to issue in markets such as this would have to have a higher cost of capital to make the issue attractive to lenders. Tax laws in this area change very fast, as evidenced by the removal of the U.S. Interest Equalization Tax and the elimination of the exemption from taxes of United States firms paying no taxes on interest payments through

---

[2]Ray Vickers, *Those Swiss Money Men* (New York: Charles Scribner's Sons, 1973), p. 47.

their international financial subsidiaries. Therefore, firms must keep constantly abreast of local changes. Investment bankers are sometimes hired to help MNCs with this task.

Investment Banking

In the United States, a dealer often holds securities for a time and then sells them. A broker, on the other hand, arranges sales and earns a commission for his work. The investment banker performs the functions of both a broker and a dealer on a larger scale. This is also true internationally, but there are some differences.

In countries where the banking system is important in controlling the issue of securities, it is also important in the selling of securities. In Belgium, bankers can act as a broker or a dealer but not as both. In Germany, banks are admitted as dealers on the stock exchange. However, to do business with the banks, brokers must have governmental permission.

Some countries use the term "jobber." Jobber is applied to an individual who performs duties similar to those of the dealer. However, the jobber is different from the dealer in that he does not work directly with the public. In England, the broker acts as an agent for a customer to aid in locating the best price he can. He accomplishes this by dealing with a jobber whose main function is to buy and sell securities.

Most countries endeavor to segment dealers and brokers. Some countries do not allow firms who engage in both functions to deal with each other. There are exceptions, of course. The typical situation, though, is that a firm must choose which function it wishes to perform. Separation of the broker and dealer is advantageous in that the chance for manipulation of securities is reduced. However, in separating functions, some efficiency is usually lost.

In recent years, investment bankers have played an icreasingly important and complex role in the floatation of international equities and bonds. Domestic balance-of-payments problems, monetary fluctuations, intricate international taxation considerations, broad fluctuations and differentials in interest rates, devaluation, revaluation, and domestic limitations upon the capital markets are some of the factors underlying the extension of the investment banker's domain. Governments and private firms depend upon the investment banker not only for his expertise in the floatation of securities, but also for his concommitant expertise in such diverse areas as taxation and leasing.

The term "investment banker," while apparently referring to a singular institution, often refers to an underwriting syndicate. The individual investment banker cannot afford to risk his very existence on the success of the securities of a single firm. The syndicate involves the combination of many investment houses sharing the risks of issuance over a broader area. Another advantage of syndication is that the individual security can be sold simultaneously over a much larger market area.

The single most important function of investment bankers is assisting in public bond sales. This assistance commences long before the actual floatation of the bond issue. The investment banker will create a package for his client consisting of alternatives chosen to meet the needs of the market and of the issuer. Perhaps the investment banker will advise his client that due to current world monetary conditions, the issue should be denominated in a quasi currency (for example, Units of Account). The denomination of the issue in terms of a UOA would minimize (in the eyes of the banker) the risk of broad fluctuations in the value of the issue. The inclusion of several types of currencies (for example, French francs, Dutch guilders, American dollars) can be an effective risk minimization tool for the investment banker.

Another function of the investment banker is the arrangement of equity financing. The investment banker may either acquire the issue outright or agree to sell the issue for a specified charge. Naturally, the more he does or the greater amount of risks he takes, the more he must charge.

The role of intermediary is an important function of the investment banker. Often the investment banker will seek a private placement for the securities of a small firm without the prestige or capital base to support a public stock or bond floatation. The investment banker acting as broker arranges a private placement of the securities with a pension fund or insurance company in return for a finder's fee. Increasingly, the investment banker has assumed the role of broker with the growing importance of institutions. The large insurance companies and pension funds circumvent the market and perhaps avoid some of the costs associated with the public market for funds. This trend could be reversed with the advent of negotiated commissions but private placement via the investment banker should still maintain advantages vis-à-vis the public stock market.

The investment banker also assists small firms and, to a degree, large firms needing a new partner in a foreign country. The smaller firms do not possess the managerial or financial capacity to search for a partner in a joint venture or develop a foreign market without the valuable experience and contacts of the international investment banker. The banker can locate a suitable partner, acquire the requisite funds and assist the firm in the introductory phases of the new enterprise. Traditionally, the investment banker was concerned primarily with the floatations of securities, while the counseling of clients as to practicality of a joint venture, monetary and political conditions, and other intelligence were more minor ingredients of the primary service.

However, the heretofore ancillary services were frequently requested by the smaller firms. It was a very profitable service the investment banker could provide utilizing the same assets it already possessed, so the banker readily accepted these requests.

The primary role of the investment banker is to serve as intermediary between those firms requiring capital and those who wish to invest their "excess" funds. While the banker has been cognizant of his talents, he has often utilized them only in the context of performing his primary function. As the investment banker has become more aware of the demand for his talents, he has moved into such areas as leasing, trading in the international monetary markets, and maintaining a house position in many currencies, bonds, and equities.

Underwriting

Investment bankers in the United States can accept the risks associated with price fluctuations of a bond issue by "underwriting" that issue. They guarantee the sale at a fixed price by purchasing and distributing new securities of individual companies. Most other countries also have some form of underwriting employed in their markets.

Many countries have their bond issues underwritten by a consortium of banks. These countries are primarily smaller countries that rely to a great extent on control of the market to maintain market stability. In these countries, a good relationship with the banking industry is very beneficial.

Other countries employ what is called subunderwriting. Subunderwriters, along with the issuing houses, aid in allocating resources and evaluating requests for funds from a long-term point of view. They also help issuing houses in selecting companies to underwrite. Subunderwriting in Australia is performed mainly by pension funds and insurance companies. In England, a merchant bank, which issues large volumes of securities, uses subunderwriting to guard itself against loss due to the change in market price from the date of issuance to the date of sale.

Competition

We have examined some of the functions of the investment banker, but let us now look more closely at the unique difficulties confronting the international investment bankers. Historically, the United States inflation rate has not usually been a major market depressant. However, many countries, particularly in Latin America, experience very high rates of inflation which effectively retard any broad appeal of the country as a source of funds.

Thus, the job of the investment banker is further complicated when he attempts to raise funds in international markets. When analyzing the optimal market for a security, a large portion of the world market must be ignored or at least highly discounted due to inflationary considerations. There are, however, many other restrictions upon the world market for funds. Often countries upset over balance of payment problems will initiate controls to alter the current trends in capital flows. The United States did this in 1964 with its "interest equalization" tax. West Germany also restricted capital flows by requiring deposits in noninterest-bearing accounts to match a proportion of foreign money raised abroad. These are but two examples. The development of similar monetary regulations across a broad spectrum of countries can severely restrict a major portion of the world as a market for funds. The investment banker and his clients operating in the world market can suddenly be faced with a drastic alteration of the constraints of the market and, as a result, may no longer be able to compete in a particular area.

Recent developments in the investment banking field have created increasing competition for the international investment banker. In France, recent reforms have allowed the commercial banker to invest in the equity of corporations. This has resulted in the entrance of the commercial bank into many fields reserved for the investment banker. West Germany, also, has allowed many of its financial institutions to carry on the function of an investment banker. The larger German banks are active in every field of investment banking including underwriting and stock brokerage transactions, finding new acquisitions for clients, and assisting in mergers. In fact, the three largest banks have vast holdings in equity to the point of effective control of many German companies. German banks actively support the secondary market for funds—a function most often associated with the investment banker.

The banks of Italy, the Netherlands, and Switzerland have also become increasingly active in the international investment banking field. In the United Kingdom, the merchant banker has become a significant factor in the competition among international investment bankers. The English banker has the expertise required for investment banking and, because of the lack of funds in Great Britain, has sought to fulfill the role of broker in the international market for funds—further increasing the competition among bankers vying for a given amount of business. It seems that not only is the market complex, but the competition is becoming more strenuous. The demand for international assistance in raising capital has created a growing variety of financial institutions willing to assist.

In summary, the international investment banker must contend with the risks confronting the domestic investment banker plus the pervasive risk associated with the international investment environment. The international investment banker must deal with nationalistic economic and monetary policy, vagaries of the world monetary values, and the often underdeveloped condition of security markets. When markets begin to develop, the international investment banker must compete not only with his fellow investment bankers, but with a growing number of commercial banks, domiciled in foreign markets, that are entering fields traditionally reserved for the investment banker. Nevertheless, the very complexity and challenge of the international markets for funds has created the need for the investment banker with a knowledge and feel for the world market. The experience and success of the investment banker in dealing with international problems has ensured his continued survival.

Conclusion

The process of issuing bonds and stocks on an international basis carries with it the normal requirements and problems found in issuing domestically, plus a larger number of problems unique to the international issue.

This chapter has focused on where the multinational corporation goes for international funds outside the realm of the parent's headquarters, the risks that ensue in crossing national borders, and the restrictions—whether governmental or self-imposed—that multinationals might want to observe when they approach international capital markets. Investment bankers and other financial middlemen are sometimes available to help. The development banks provide capital on very favorable terms, but the loans are hard to obtain. Investment bankers can help find other sources, but they charge for their services and the funds are often expensive.

In the final summation, long-term financing of international operations has helped multinationals secure sources of funds with which they conduct their global operations. The effort to reach these sources can be expensive and still result in risks which firms do not face domestically. It has also forced them to look carefully at the socioeconomic climate where they wish to operate. Eurobond and Euroequities have helped reduce risks and ease market entry, but the added complexities still contain a certain amount of added risks. However, as long as overseas returns remain as high as they have been, these added problems seem to be worthwhile.

Bibliography

Adler, Michael, and Bernard Dumas, "Optimal International Acquisitions." *Journal of Finance,* March 1975, pp. 1–19.

Business International Corporation. *Financing Foreign Operations.* Current issues.

Carleton, Willard. "An Analytical Model for Long-Range Financial Planning." *Journal of Finance,* May 1970, pp. 291–315.

Carter, E. Eugene. *Portfolio Aspects of Corporate Capital Budgets.* Boston: D. C. Heath and Company, 1974.

Dawson, Steven. "Eurobond Currency Selection: Hindsight." *Financial Executive,* November 1973, pp. 72–73.

de Faro, Clovis, and James Jucker, "The Impact of Inflation and Devaluation on the Selection of an International Borrowing Source." *Journal of International Business Studies,* Fall 1973, pp. 97–104.

Dufey, Gunter. *The Eurobond Market.* Seattle: University of Washington, Graduate School of Business, 1969.

———. "The Euro-Bond Market: Its Significance for International Financial Managers." *Journal of International Business Studies,* Summer 1970, pp. 65–81.

Einzig, Paul. *The Euro-Bond Market.* New York: St. Martin's Press, Inc., 1969.

Ellis, C. Allen, and John Wadsworth, Jr. "United States Corporations and the International Capital Market Abroad." *Financial Analysts Journal,* May-June 1966, pp. 169–75.

Elman, Lee. "Facts of Life About the Integration of National Capital Markets." *Journal of Money, Credit and Banking,* August 1969, p. 319.

Grubel, Herbert, and Kenneth Fadner, "The Interdependence of International Equity Markets." *Journal of Finance,* March 1971, pp. 89–94.

Heller, H. Robert. "Borrowers in International Capital Markets." *The National Banking Review,* September 1966, pp. 81–87.

Houk, J. T. Dock. *Financing and Problems of Development Banking.* New York: Praeger Publishers, Inc., 1966.

Kohers, Theodor. "The Effect of Multinational Operations on the Cost of Equity Capital of U.S. Corporations: An Empirical Study." *Management International Review,* no. 2-3, 1975, pp. 121–24.

Kramer, Gerald. "Borrowing on the International Capital Markets." *Columbia Journal of World Business,* January 1974, pp. 73–77.

Lees, Francis, and Maximo Eng, *International Financial Markets.* New York: Praeger Publishers, Inc., 1975.

Lessard, Donald. "World, Country and Industry Relationships in Equity Returns: Implications for Risk Reduction through International Diversification." *Financial Analysts Journal,* January-February 1976, pp. 32–38.

———. "World, National, and Industry Factors Affecting Equity Returns." *Journal of Finance,* May 1974, pp. 379–91.

Lusztig, Peter, and Bernhard Schwab, "Units of Accounting and the International Bond Market." *Columbia Journal of World Business,* Spring 1975, p. 75.

Mendelson, Morris. "The Eurobond and Capital Market Integration." *Journal of Finance,* March 1972, pp. 110–26.

Myers, Stewart, and Gerald Pogue, "A Programming Approach to Corporate Financial Management." *Journal of Finance,* May 1974, pp. 175–96.

Nehrt, Lee. *International Finance for Multinational Business.* 2nd ed. Scranton, Pa.: Intext, Inc., 1972. pp. 363–590.

Panton, D., V. Lessig, and O. M. Joy, "Comovement of International Equity Markets: A Taxonomic Approach." *Journal of Financial and Quantitative Analysis.* September 1976, pp. 415–32.

Park, Yoon. *The Euro-Bond Market: Function and Structure.* New York: Praeger Publishers, Inc., 1974.

Penzkofer, P. "Character and Structure of the Euro-Capital Market." *Management International Review,* no. 1, 1969, p. 107.

Rodriguez, Rita, and Eugene Carter, *International Financial Management.* Englewood Cliffs, N.J.: Prentice-Hall, Inc., 1976. pp. 461–580.

Solnik, Bruno. *European Capital Markets.* Lexington, Mass.: D. C. Heath/Lexington Books, 1973.

Vickers, Ray. *Those Swiss Money Men.* New York: Charles Scribner's Sons, 1973.

Wai, U. Tan, and H. T. Patrick. "Stock and Bond Issues and Capital Markets in Less Developed Countries." *IMF Staff Papers,* July 1973, pp. 253–317.

Waterman, Marvin. "Capital Sources for Multinational Companies." *Financial Executive,* May 1968, pp. 25–42.

Williams, David. "The Development of Capital Markets in Europe." *IMF Staff Papers,* March 1965, pp. 37–61.

Zinn, Eberhard. "The International Money and Capital Market of the Euro-Currencies." *European Business,* April 1969, p. 59.

```
12121212121212121212121212121212121212121212121212121212121212121212121212
12121212121212121212121212121212121212121212121212121212121212121212121212
121212121212121212121212121    12121    121    121    121212121212121212121212
1212121212121212121212121212    212    2121    121    121212121212121212121212
12121212121212121212121212121    1    12121    121    121212121212121212121212
121212121212121212121212121212       212121    121    121212121212121212121212
1212121212121212121212121212121    1212121    121    121212121212121212121212
121212121212121212121212121212       212121    121    121212121212121212121212
12121212121212121212121212121    1    12121    121    121212121212121212121212
1212121212121212121212121212    212    2121    121    121212121212121212121212
121212121212121212121212121    12121    121    121    121212121212121212121212
12121212121212121212121212121212121212121212121212121212121212121212121212
12121212121212121212121212121212121212121212121212121212121212121212121212
```

Leasing*

Leases are usually written so that the lessor will charge enough to cover all his risks and still make a profit. In fact, this is often cited as the major disadvantage of a domestic lease; namely, that the lessor's profit means that the costs to the lessee are often greater than the benefits. But there is an important distinction that needs to be made between domestic business and business done between parties of different countries. In the latter case, the risks of the two parties are *not* necessarily the same. Whenever the lessor has *fewer* risks than the lessee, he is able to charge less since he need not charge for those risks that only his client faces. In this way, the client can pay a leasing charge that ignores some of his risks.

Expropriation

To be specific, the decision to make a direct foreign investment involves considering at least two basic risks which domestic investments do not have: expropriation and devaluation. In each of these areas, international leasing is unique in that it can sometimes be used to reduce, if not eliminate, some risks at no cost. Expropriation, for example, is usually a major concern in any country being considered

*Most of the material in this chapter was originally published by the author and Saeed Samiee-Esfahani in the *Journal of International Business Studies,* Fall 1974, pp. 87–90.

for investment outside Western Europe, North America, and Japan—especially if the country has had a history of nationalizing foreign corporate properties. Leasing can ease investors' concern over expropriation and open the road for the mulitnational enterprise to invest in almost every country where it is welcome. Furthermore, governments of developing countries who solicit direct foreign investment usually offer concessions to the foreign investors in several ways. One such benefit is making available government-owned land and/or buildings to the foreign investor through leasing at bargain prices. In countries where such government-sponsored benefits do not exist, the multinational corporation may still minimize its initial investment by seeking a lease on the land and buildings through local private sources.

In leasing equipment and machinery in a developing economy, however, there is a very good chance that a substantial portion of the required merchandise will not be locally available. The multinational firm can often solve this problem by purchasing the necessary equipment elsewhere, selling it to a local leasing firm, and leasing it back.

Leasing simply reduces the risk of expropriation of company assets by the foreign government. Should an expropriation take place, only the subsidiary's current assets will be in danger, and current assets can be kept at a minimum level through shifting of funds to more reliable subsidiaries. Moreover, a low level of assets should not be a problem for the subsidiary, since it can make use of its parent company's reputation as guarantees for lease payments. At the same time, the parent company may find it suitable to purchase the leased machinery and equipment after the lease terms have expired at substantially lower prices than their actual market value. This action is permissible in many instances because many countries lack laws and regulations regarding leasing. Also, in many developing countries where tax laws and their enforcement are rather lethargic, the lessee might be able to enjoy maximum lease payment deductions as well as being able to purchase the machinery and equipment after the lease has run out.

The important point is that a locally based lessor usually does not need to worry about his own government "expropriating" his assets so he need not add much to his leasing charge to cover that risk. But if his client is not a local citizen, then the risk (had the client purchased the asset rather than leased it) might very well be great enough that the client would be willing to pay a substantial amount to eliminate it. In other words, the lessor can provide a risk-reduction service at very little cost (or risk) to himself.

Devaluation

A second unique risk involved in international operations is currency devaluation. Devaluation of local currency is not limited to developing economies and is rather widespread among all countries. Due to recent states of flux in the currency exchange market and international monetary imbalances, changes in currency values have become an even larger threat to the operations of the multinational corporation.

It is possible to reduce the cost of a devaluation if the purchased asset is being paid for over a long period of time with the weak currency that is obtained from loan arrangements which can also be repaid in weak currencies. But such financing arrangements are rare. More often, the asset is purchased with a strong currency immediately —and usually with money that must eventually be replaced in strong currencies.

The parent company can much more easily minimize such costs, however, if some or all of its subsidiary's assets are leased and the contract calls for payments in the currency which is weak. Thus, should a devaluation occur, the payments are actually less than previously stated in terms of the hard currency.

Devaluation risks, therefore, can be reduced with little extra cost by leasing from a local firm. A local lessor—especially of land or locally produced assets—is not particularly worried about a local devaluation. In fact, he usually prefers that the contract be stated in terms that require payments in his country's currency—even if that currency may be devalued from time to time. After all, the internal value of the money and most of what it is used for would remain much the same for him regardless of whether or not a devaluation occurred. So he will not charge much for a risk which is unimportant to him even though it is of potentially great importance to his international clients.

Tax Aspects

In addition to reducing the risk of expropriations and devaluations, leasing may also provide an international firm with an opportunity to reduce its total tax obligations. As stated earlier, a large number of countries do not have any laws and regulations regarding leasing and its treatment as a business expense. Those countries, by default or otherwise, obviously permit firms to reduce their taxes. But even in countries which do restrict the use of leasing for tax purposes, there are often ways of getting around some of the existing laws. In Sweden, for example, an end-of-lease purchase is considered to be installment buying and, hence, leasing payments are not a legitimate "business expense." Some leasing companies, however, have gotten around this difficulty by selling the equipment back to the manufacturer, who in turn resells the equipment to the original lessee. The lessee then runs no risk of losing his tax gains, and equipment that is generally depreciated for over a five-year period has been written off by the lessor in three years.

Governments sometimes also provide "incentives" to firms using leases. In France, for example, leasing has actually been promoted by the government in times of tight money. The government has made loans of 200 francs for every 100 francs put up by a lessor if he is French. In such a case, leasing is not only an instrument enabling the subsidiary to avoid unique risks, but it is a way of using the equipment at a possible savings (depending upon the interest rate charged by the government—a rate that is generally lower than the market rate —and upon the willingness of the lessor to pass on some of this governmental subsidy by charging less).

The net result of these tax and legal aspects is that leasing firms may be able to provide an asset for an international firm's use at an after-tax cost which is below any other alternative.

Additional Considerations

Besides risk and tax reduction, there may be other reasons for leasing abroad—reasons that, by their very nature, do not exist domestically. To be more specific, while some countries have begun placing tighter restrictions on local borrowing by foreign companies—especially for expansion—or have started curtailing foreign direct investments in other ways, they typically do not prohibit leasing. (Germany, for example, now requires prior approval for investment but not for leasing.)

Additionally, balance of payment problems have forced some countries to prohibit the purchase and importation of equipment into their countries. Exceptions have been made, however, if the import is to be leased. Justification for these exceptions is usually based upon the premise that "a country's balance of payments is far less affected by remittance of rental for leased equipment than [by] payment for imports."[1] But whatever the justification is, the fact remains that leasing may be more desirable—even essential—overseas even when it is not domestically.

Conclusions

It is not suggested that leasing is a better alternative in all instances and for all of the subsidiaries of a multinational firm. It is, however, recommended that leasing be considered as an alternative and that the final decision should be based on a thorough analysis of all factors.

---

[1] *Business International,* April 6, 1973, p. 110.

In addition to the factors which are considered domestically, there may be international tax and other benefits in leasing. Furthermore, an international firm (whether based in the United States or abroad) must consider the value of reducing the impact of a threatened expropriation or devaluation. As this chapter points out, it might be possible to reduce these two risks with a lease which makes no extra charges for doing so. The final decision to lease or not, however, would depend upon the willingness of the parent company and/or its subsidiary to be exposed to these risks. The leasing costs may still outweigh the advantages they provide, but a lease is certainly worthy of consideration —especially if you are doing business internationally. It is possible that leasing may be the best alternative abroad even when it is not at home!

Bibliography

"International Leasing: Filling Equipment Needs of Capital-Short Customers Around the World." *Business Abroad,* May 1970, p. 11.

Parker, George, and Henry Miller, "The Lease: Use Without Ownership." *Columbia Journal of World Business,* September-October 1970, pp. 77–82.

Ricks, David, and Saeed Samiee-Esfahani, "Leasing: It May Be Right Abroad Even When It Is Not At Home." *Journal of International Business Studies,* Fall 1974, pp. 87–91.

Profit Remission and Retained Earnings Policy

It is generally considered good business domestically to have a consistent and predictable dividend policy. The absolute amount or the percentage of earnings paid out is often fixed in advance so that investors know "what they are buying." However, it is also generally considered good business domestically to have a retained earnings policy to keep all the funds that can be used more profitably by the firm than by the stockholders. The trouble is that such a policy often conflicts with dividend policy unless the dividend policy is simply to pay out whatever is not optimally retained. Such a dividend policy is a bit too uncertain and complex for many potential investors so many firms seek some suboptimal compromise.

All this may sound complicated, but it is nothing compared to the problems of establishing and living with the policies in multinational operations. It is true that most subsidiaries have only one stockholder (the parent firm) so it is easier to determine the opportunities of the stockholder, but MNCs have many more variables and risks to consider.

This chapter will discuss how the financial variables of the multinational's profit-remittance decision compare with the domestic variables. It will also look at how the decision to remit profits is made and then examine differences in national and firm policies. While the purpose of this chapter is the discussion of fund remittances as they apply to a firm's distribution of earnings, primary emphasis will be on dividends. This is because dividends are the most important method utilized by firms to distribute earnings. Also to be considered, however, are the alternative ways that the parent is the recipient of a subsidiary's earnings.

Factors for Consideration

The most important considerations given to how domestic earnings are distributed are:

1. The company's earnings record and its future prospects
2. The company's dividend record
3. The company's cash needs
4. The needs and expectations of stockholders

International guidelines on profit remittance—especially dividend policy—are similar to domestic ones. One fundamental guideline is to reduce risks by paying out unneeded funds. This principle is applied both domestically and internationally. The difference is that, since most foreign operations seem riskier, MNCs generally prefer larger remittances from abroad—often as soon as possible. MNCs don't want to have to worry about currency devaluations or governmental restrictions on repatriation.

Because of the additional uncertainties and risk factors in a foreign environment, the parent may expect almost total remittance of profits from the subsidiary. This is seen as a subsidiary's obligatory compensation to the parent for the parent's capital investment being tied up in a foreign risk environment. In other cases, though, the parent may be satisfied with reinvestment of the earnings of subsidiaries back into the subsidiary for expansion needs. The parent may feel that the continued growth and stability of its subsidiaries do the most to reflect the overall corporate strength to stockholders and potential stockholders.

A parental requirement to have all earnings remitted in order to reduce exposure is not always popular with the various subsidiaries, of course. The subsidiary may feel that those funds should be reinvested in the subsidiary. Otherwise, capital expansion projects may be delayed and the subsidiary may have to borrow funds locally at high rates of interest. Usually some sort of compromise is necessary. It is generally better to have some flexibility in remittance requirements in order to best meet the needs of parent and all subsidiaries of the MNC.

In a study by David B. Zenoff of thirty of the United States' largest multinational companies, it was agreed by all the firms that the final decision as to the amount of foreign earnings to be remitted to the parent should be the parent's.[1] In this way, subsidiaries are aware that profits are the property of the owners who made the initial investments and do not automatically belong to the subsidiary to be treated independently of the whole corporation. Not only is the parent able to maintain better control of worldwide operations when the decision on remittance is its own, but each subsidiary is also "encouraged" to work more clearly toward overall company objectives.

Zenoff found that the parent company's decision on the amount of earnings to be remitted is dependent upon the added problems, risks, and uncertainties perceived in the foreign environment.[2] In particular, executives considered how much more *information* was needed, how reliable and available it was, and how comfortable they would feel using it. They also considered the repercussions of failing to adequately protect the firm from currency or political problems. The general tendency is to reduce a firm's exposure abroad by remitting a subsidiary's profits.

Companies may also minimize their exposures by limiting initial capital investment. This is done by insisting that the foreign subsidiary provide its own funds through extensive local borrowing. The pros and cons of this strategy were the subject of chapter 10.

Another way to reduce the risks of funding overseas operations is to publicly announce that such investments would result in steady repayments. If the host government approves, then such remittances should proceed as scheduled. Generally, governments prefer prior agreement and steady money flows.

One of the most popular rules of thumb is for foreign subsidiaries to keep excess funds only to the extent that they meet working capital requirements. The amount of funds actually remitted may exceed the otherwise ordinary amount, when (1) there is an imminent danger of devaluation of currency in the host country; (2) the tax factors are such that distributed earnings are taxed at a lower rate than retained earnings in the host country, or the parent country has some special advantage in the way of foreign tax credits; and/or (3) the government of the host country imposes few or no restrictions on the amount of funds repatriated.

The amount remitted may be less than usual in those situations where (1) the subsidiary has a pressing need for funds that are either unobtainable or obtainable only from local foreign sources at exorbi-

---

[1]David Zenoff, "Profitable, Fast Growing, but Still the Stepchild," *Columbia Journal of World Business*, July-August 1967, pp. 51–56.

[2]David Zenoff, "Remitting Funds From Foreign Affiliates," *Financial Executive*, March 1968, p. 46.

tant interest rates, (2) the parent views reinvestment of a local's earnings as more important for overall company growth, (3) the host country has a favorable balance-of-payments position so there is a possibility of currency value appreciation, and/or (4) the total tax implications are such that there is a benefit to the multinational to reinvest earnings at the local level.

Taxes

The impact of taxes has been frequently mentioned, but its importance will depend upon a number of factors.[3] The Zenoff study found that taxes were the single most important criteria of analysis in determining the remittance policies of twenty-five percent of the companies surveyed. These companies made every effort to minimize their total tax burden. For thirty-five percent of the companies, tax aspects were of about equal importance to such considerations as cash needs and perceived currency risks. For a little more than twenty percent of the companies, paying taxes in the United States on dividend income received from abroad was considered a fact of doing business internationally. Such companies merely tried to avoid penalty taxes, which are taxes resulting from paying too large a dividend or failing to pay a required dividend. Finally, for a few multinational firms, the tax variable was assigned a relatively low degree of importance on the dividend decision.[4]

The latter point of view was taken primarily by those multinational firms whose priorities were for growth through retention of earnings. With reinvestment of earnings, the company may feel that a subsidiary's ability to show its independence and stability is important enough that neither the tax variables nor the threat of foreign exchange losses are initially considered crucial. By being independent, the subsidiary may show its value to stockholders.

Where taxes are the most important criteria or are equally important with respect to both the subsidiary's fund requirements and the threat of devaluation, the effect of local tax laws may be to encourage the corporate manager to remit a larger amount of dividends than would ordinarily be the case. In Germany, for example, retained earnings are taxed at a rate of fifty-one percent, while distributed earnings are only subject to a fifteen-percent tax rate. Although there is a fifteen-percent withholding tax on declared dividends, there may still be an important tax advantage for firms to repatriate everything pos-

---

[3]The reader is reminded that a general background to the role of taxes in international finance was the subject of chapter 2. This section looks specifically at the role of taxes in determining dividend remittance policy.

[4]Zenoff, "Remitting Funds From Foreign Affiliates," p. 50.

sible from Germany and then meet the subsidiary's need for funds with loans from the parent or through local borrowings.

A more recent study by Walter Ness found that United States tax laws usually encourage the accumulation of earnings in low-tax countries unless special tax credit conditions exist.[5] Managers giving considerable attention to taxes may be aware of all the added risks of leaving profits abroad, but may feel that it is worthwhile if United States tax liabilities can be adequately deferred or reduced.

Domestic Policy

Another consideration given to international fund remittance decisions is the parent payout plan as exercised in the home country. The parent payout ratio may be a good guide to follow for these reasons: (1) It assures both the subsidiary manager and the multinational manager that an established amount of funds will be contributed to the worldwide pool from each subsidiary; (2) the subsidiary is demonstrating its contribution to the success of the multinational in a concrete, measurable way; and (3) planning to maintain a subsidiary's adequate fund position may be easier since the manager knows that a certain proportion of earnings will be remitted to the parent.

Joint Ventures

Everything becomes even more complicated if the overseas investment is a joint venture. The partner may not have the same risks or interests. If it is a local firm, for example, it may not feel concerned with possible currency changes so it may be more inclined to retain more earnings. The local partner certainly has no special reason for trying to maximize the MNC's global operations.

Most foreign firms prefer a higher payout ratio than is normal in the United States. This has potential problems if both partners want to follow their respective home business practices. A compromise may be possible, but usually no one is happy. Conflict is not that common only because the United States firms that are interested in reducing international risks by having higher than normal United States payouts are those more likely to accept a partner that also wants the payout which is high by United States standards. It is the MNC that fails to talk over dividend policy with a potential partner that gets into problems later.

---

[5]Walter Ness, "U.S. Corporate Income Taxation, and the Dividend Remission Policy of Multinational Corporations," *Journal of International Business Studies*, Spring 1975, p. 67.

Methods of Remittance

How much to remit and how to remit are two separate questions. The previous discussion centered on the quantity question. Let us now turn to the decision of *how* to make the remittance.

Although dividends are the most important vehicle for profit remission in multinational business, alternative methods such as royalties and fees have grown in relative importance. The actual remittance of profits by methods other than through dividends is determined by:

1. The value of the services and benefits provided the foreign subsidiary
2. The amount allowed by foreign taxing authorities as deductible business expenses
3. The total amount of contribution to the overhead of the international division desired from overseas operations, pro-rated to each subsidiary
4. The overall corporate tax picture, including the availability of foreign tax credits and the possibilities of remitting funds in the form of dividends

Dividends are not the main remittance form when the host country restricts fund flows from the country or when taxes on dividend payments are high. In most countries, it costs more to remit with dividends because they must be paid out of after-tax earnings. Fees, royalties, and interest payments, on the other hand, are normally allowable as a business expense against taxes. These latter forms of remittance are considered part of the cost of doing business in the host country and represent the charge by the parent company of rendering services, advice, and assistance to the subsidiary. The royalties and fees methods of profit remittances are desirable in situations where there are restrictions on dividend outlay, where the tax benefits are maximized, or where some measure is sought of a parent's degree of involvement with its subsidiaries.

Use of repayment on loans and interest payments on loans outstanding can often minimize taxes or political pressures. The host country may dislike dividend remittances but be more lenient when the company "remits" in the form of repayment of its obligations (so loans are often made with high interest rates). Thus, the subsidiary is both reducing its indebtedness to the parent and providing that parent with funds for worldwide operations.

One additional method of remitting funds internationally is through transfer pricing. In countries that impose restrictions on dividends and other remittance forms, transfer prices may be the only way to repatriate funds. Transfer pricing is done by having the parent set the prices of goods bought and sold between its organizations such that profits show up where desired. If funds are desired in one country, the organization there pays less for supplies and charges more for its products. This method, of course, is not without its problems. Host countries don't like such actions and managers often feel uncomfortable.[6] Overuse may result in expropriation or management disharmony. Furthermore, such a pricing strategy is totally unacceptable to partners if the firm is a joint venture.

General Patterns

Remittance decisions are highly dependent upon the company and the countries involved. However, general characteristics seem to prevail.[7] For those companies that are experienced in international operations, have a large number of subsidiaries, and have a large amount of total earnings contributed by foreign subsidiaries, the remittance decision is usually closely related to a predetermined target percentage. For those companies that are not as experienced in international operations, the remittance plan is more often formulated on the basis of those variables already considered and a more thorough analysis is given to the individual variables.

There appears also to be some correlation with the level of development of a country and its degree of remittance restriction. The more-developed countries usually have a steadier position in currency (though not always) and are usually less concerned about funds leaving the country. The less-developed countries are often troubled by balance-of-payments difficulties and are more likely to impose some type of control or restraint on dividend remittances.

Summary

Both domestic and international firms strive to optimize long-run objectives by considering all aspects related to dividends and profit remission. Many of the variables, such as tax considerations, are of concern to both groups. However, the international firms have more risks, more complexities, and more uncertainties to deal with. Therefore, they are more tempted to remit earnings faster. Tax credits and special situations sometimes discourage this, but not indefinitely. Furthermore, some of these firms find political barriers to dividend payments. These firms must derive alternative—sometimes even artificial—methods of remitting funds. Royalties, fees, and loans with high interest rates are often used. Transfer pricing is another possibility.

---

[6] For a complete discussion on transfer pricing, see James Shulman, "When the Price is Wrong by Design," *Columbia Journal of World Business,* May-June 1967, p. 69.

[7] David Zenoff and Jack Zwick, *International Financial Management* (Englewood Cliffs, N.J.: Prentice-Hall, Inc., 1969), p. 418.

The entire fund remittance problem can actually be summarized in four stages. This decision making sequence is presented in Table 13-1. The first stage involves the determination of whether or not funds should be remitted. It is necessary to consider obligations to the parent company as well as the potential value remitted funds would have elsewhere.

The second stage involves the determination of how much should be remitted. Many factors come into play here, as listed. The third stage is to select the form for remittance. The best form will depend upon such things as company practice, tax regulations, and previous actions. Finally, the fourth stage is the synthesis and resultant decision.

TABLE 13-1 Sequence of Analysis and Decisions

Stage 1 *Should funds be remitted?* *Reasons for:*	*Stage 2* *How much should be remitted?* *Depends on:*	*Stage 3* *What forms of remittance?* *Depends on:*	*Stage 4* *Synthesis*
To pay for use of company-owned resources	Amount invested or loaned	Industry and company practice	
	Parent company's expectations	Tax implications	
Technology	Parent company's objectives	Organization and structure	
Invested capital	Local and U.S. tax regulations, rates and credits	Percentage of equity possessed	Synthesis and final decision
Property rights	Company and industry practice	Alternative remittance forms permitted by government	
Loans	Parent company's attitude toward risk	Establishment of remittance record	
To effect better worldwide deployment of funds	Local government regulations U.S. government regulations		
To obtain higher rate of return	Cost and availability of funds from external sources		
To assure accessibility	Fund requirements of affiliate and worldwide company		
To minimize risks			

SOURCE: David B. Zenoff and Jack Zwick, *International Financial Management*, (Englewood Cliffs, N.J.: Prentice-Hall, Inc., 1969), p. 438.

Bibliography

Greene, James. *The Conference Board Record,* October 1969, pp. 43–48.

Keegan, Warren. "Multinational Pricing: How Far is Arm's Length?" *Columbia Journal of World Business,* May-June 1969, pp. 57–66.

Ness, Walter. "U.S. Corporate Income Taxation, and the Dividend Remission Policy of Multinational Corporations." *Journal of Internatinal Business Studies,* Spring 1975, pp. 67–77.

Obersteiner, Erich. "Should The Foreign Affiliate Remit Dividends or Reinvest?" *Financial Management,* Spring 1973, pp. 88–93.

Polk, Judd, Irene Meister, and Lawrence Veit, *U.S. Production Abroad and the Balance of Payments: A Survey of Corporate Investment Experience.* New York: National Industrial Conference Board, 1966.

Shulman, James. "When the Price is Wrong—By Design." *Columbia Journal of World Business,* May-June 1967, pp. 69–76.

Summa, Donald. "Remittances by U.S. Owned Foreign Corporations: Tax Considerations." *Columbia Journal of World Business,* Summer 1975, pp. 40–45.

Zenoff, David. "Profitable, Fast-Growing, but Still the Stepchild." *Columbia Journal of World Business,* July-August 1967, pp. 51–56.

———. "Remittance Policies of U.S. Subsidiaries in Europe." *The Banker,* March 1967, pp. 418–27.

———. "Remitting Funds from Foreign Affiliates." *Financial Executive,* March 1968, pp. 46–63.

———, and Jack Zwick, *International Financial Management.* Englewood Cliffs, N.J.: Prentice-Hall, Inc., 1969. pp. 412–40.

Part Five

MERGERS AND ACQUISITIONS

```
14141414141414141414141414141414141414141414141414141414141414141414141414
14141414141414141414141414141414141414141414141414141414141414141414141414
141414141414141414141   14141   141   141   141414141414I   14141414141414141414
1414141414141414141414   414   4141   1414   41414141414   414141414141414141414
14141414141414141414141   1   14141   14141   141414141   141414141414141414141414
141414141414141414141414      414141   141414   4141414   4141414141414141414141414
1414141414141414141414141   1414141   1414141   14141   1414141414141414141414141414
141414141414141414141414      414141   14141414   414   414141414141414141414141414
14141414141414141414141   1   14141   141414141   1   1414141414141414141414141414
1414141414141414141414   414   4141   1414141414      41414141414141414141414141414
141414141414141414141   14141   141   14141414141   141414141414141414141414141414
14141414141414141414141414141414141414141414141414141414141414141414141414
14141414141414141414141414141414141414141414141414141414141414141414141414
```

Mergers and Acquisitions

INTERNATIONAL acquisition is no newcomer to world business. However, it has atracted great attention and generated much interest in the 1950s and 60s as the United States passed through the import-export and portfolio investment stages to the direct foreign investment stage of international business. Today, United States direct investment abroad accounts for over forty billion dollars and involves the movement of huge blocks of money, physical capital, and management expertise into entirely different foreign constraint sets.

Wholly owned subsidiaries and joint ventures have become the major vehicles of international business involvement. To a great extent, corporations approach the acquisition of these foreign subsidiaries in the same manner they would approach a domestic acquisition. Some of the techniques and problems, such as the tender offer, or what to do with redundant labor and management forces, are exactly the same. However, the automatic application of home-grown methods, as most American managers are quite aware, leads to major problems in the international context.[1] The variable matrix to be considered is much larger, much vaguer and, in many other respects, very different. This chapter will present the variables that may be different in evaluating a potential foreign acquisition.

[1]For a description and analysis of these problems see David Ricks, Marilyn Fu, and Jeffrey Arpan, *International Business Blunders* (Columbus, Ohio: Grid, Inc., 1974).

Valuation

In screening potential acquisitions at home or abroad, there are two essential questions: "What is the company worth?" and "What will you have to pay to get it?" One might equal the other, but they seldom do. Both are exceedingly hard to quantify.

Value is a relative concept and there are many methods used to measure it including recorded or book value, market value, replacement value, assessed value, appreciated value, liquidation value, and the value of earnings potential. Earnings potential—the total expected earnings that will accrue to an asset over its life, that is, its capitalized earnings—is the most reliable indicator of value of United States firms. It quantifies the potential future earnings power of a myriad assortment of machines and ideas. Here again we must decide if by earnings we are talking of profit or the net difference in the stream of cash inflows. We are only interested in those inflows and outflows that will be a direct result of the acquisition.

Much of the method is the same in international as it is in domestic analysis. One must look at three areas: (1) the probable life span of the investment, (2) the size and value of the expected economic advantages, and (3) the projected pattern of additional investments. Examination of the pattern of economic advantages allows us to look at the advantages of other resources, other technology, the expansion of products and services, and relative efficiencies and economics of scale in addition to the higher profits from higher sales volume. In order to bring more realism to the analysis, it is also necessary to attach a probability distribution to the present value of the range of future cash flows. Such treatment in the United States will give us a good feel for the values of future injections of funds and liquidation values and the likelihood of achieving them.

Owners of prosperous firms will not accept the book value for their company, but great skill is required to put an upper bound on the price of an acquisition in any setting—domesitc or international. The most commonly used methods are to put a value on earnings or examine the capital structure in relation to industry-wide characteristics. One would look at past earnings, estimate a normal level of future earnings, and capitalize them at a rate of return commensurate with the risk structure of the industry. Unfortunately, as will be explained later in this chapter, "earnings" is largely a matter of interpretation. Income can take breath-taking swings all in accordance with "generally accepted accounting principles." What is "normal" requires careful analysis. One must be aware of growth, declines, and both secular and seasonal trends.

One can also use a present-value method by projecting future cash inflows and deducting forecasted capital additions at an adequate rate of interest. If one uses the capitalized-earnings method, the selection of normalcy is critical. With the present-value method, projected cash flow is critical. Adjustments must be made for accounting practices in picking "normal" earnings—a very difficult proposition in the international environment. Also, capitalization rates in the international environment can be driven quite high. Of course, both of these can be adjusted by attaching probability distributions to each outcome.

Capital structure considerations carry heavy weight in valuing the United States company. The degree of riskiness is partially determined by the relative amounts of debt and equity funding. The creditors are interested in debt-servicing capabilities and the equity holders want dividends and appreciation. The introduction of additional debt and fixed financial charges into the financial structure of a company makes the residual earnings more volatile. A risk measure commonly applied is the ratio of earnings before interest and taxes (EBIT) to interest and sinking fund requirements. The fact that debt capital is usually cheaper than equity capital in this country indicates that debt holders expect to be protected and are not assuming as many risks. Management must perform the balancing act by compensating higher-risk debt with higher interest rates. For our use later in this chapter, it suffices to say that earnings should be adjusted accordingly to present a more normal capital structure for the size and nature of the firm the acquisition committee might be accustomed to working with.

Regardless of the method or techniques used in valuation or the buyer's attitude toward risk, the final "worth" of an acquisition is determined in the marketplace.

> The valuation process is partly an attempt to determine economic value and partly a bargaining process in which the strength and weaknesses of the respective bargaining positions are weighted and compromised. Value rests partly upon whatever reasonable and generally acceptable judgments can be made, but largely upon personal attitudes, inclinations and circumstances surrounding the negotiations.[2]

This observation holds true domestically and internationally.

The Cunitz Model

American financial management puts heavy weight on the impact of an acquisition on the parent's earnings per share. Obviously, ac-

[2]Erich Helfert, *Valuation: Concepts and Practice* (Belmont, Calif.: Wadsworth Publishing Co., 1966), p. 87.

quiring stock of a highly levered company with good growth potential is favorable, but the firm must also provide a favorable return on investment. Short-run influences on EPS usually receive prime consideration but, in the long run, firms should be selected on the basis of present-value rate of return. Such a method of valuation—potential acquisition valuation (PAV)—has been developed by Jonathan A. Cunitz.[3] Cunitz says that in a perfect market the value of a firm's stock provides an accurate enough estimate of an acquisition price, but admits that such a market is an exception rather than the rule. Therefore, his model isolates the impact of inflation in determining growth in earnings and uses the growth due exclusively to reinvested earnings as the expected growth available from the acquisition. This normal growth is used as a prediction of future growth. Next, the price/earnings (PE) ratio is calculated (cost of acquisition/earnings). Knowing both growth rate and the PE ratio allows him to calculate the desired rate of return. "Our concern," says Cunitz, "is the growth rate of a firm and the PE necessary to take over."[4] The model neatly ties PE ratio, present value of future earnings, and the rate of return together in an easy-to-understand package. The present value of the acquisition's cost equals the present value of future earnings,

$$\frac{P_1}{E_0} = \sum_{1}^{n} \frac{1 + r_1}{1 + r_2}.$$

So, if a corporation required an after-tax rate of return of fifteen percent and the acquiree had eighteen percent, the acquirer would be willing to pay a premium to get the stock. Conversely, if the acquiree had a twelve-percent rate of return, the acquirer would want to obtain the stock at a discount.

Although Cunitz's model is intuitively appealing, it serves as an example of the potential traps of using a domestic model out of context. Cunitz adjusts earnings for inflation ascertained in the period being considered. He uses an index number for the GNP implicit price deflator and compounds inflation over the total period. This is not always possible to do in countries with poor data availability. He also assumes that inflation and growth rate are constant over the period considered. This assumption alone would make the model unworkable in many economies.

---

[3]Jonathan A. Cunitz, "Valuing Potential Acquisitions," *Financial Executive* (April 1971), p. 20.

[4]*Ibid.*, p. 24.

The Selection Process

The financial manager does not have a good, systematic model with which to evaluate international investment decisions. Once he enters the world of international business, he compounds his variable matrix dramatically. Within the United States, the social, political, and legal climate is relatively stable and he is able to concentrate on the commercial variables. With these, he is quite comfortable. He knows where to go for the information. Outside the United States, the social, political, and legal variables that were dormant in the domestic investment decision are activated. These variables are usually harder to get information on and are more difficult to quantify.

Evaluating the acquisition has to be worked up in a step-by-step, comprehensive fashion. Informal investigation should be followed by formal queries. A check list should be developed. Sales projections and manufacturing estimates must be made. Then patents, processes, resources, and legal and political setting are checked. The "are-there-any-holes?" approach can be very effective.

The central thread of acquisition planning remains clear. The company must (1) define its objectives, (2) find and screen candidates, (3) set its price criteria (that is, do the valuation), and (4) negotiate and finance the buy. In the first step the company must decide what it is looking for. It could be a greater share of the market, distribution economies, or diversifications. In the financial sense, it could be higher EPS, improved image, and subsequently higher PE multiples. The second step, finding candidates, is easy. The trick is to find *good* ones. A carefully guided search is necessary. The third stage is the valuation process. Actively traded stock provides an arms-length indicator, but this is not available in most countries. Capitalized earnings must be adjusted for additional risk factors. Additionally, earnings reported by companies in most countries are highly dependent upon local accounting conventions. These conventions can vary greatly from country to country as will be explained in the next section.

Financial Statement Problems

Many business practices commonly accepted in the United States are not very common overseas. Stock ownership, for example, will not necessarily entitle you to all the rights you get in the United States. In some countries, only three percent of your shares can be voted no matter how many shares you own and even fifty-one-percent ownership may not insure control. The directors may be able to delegate all management power to one outsider. Voting trusts are often unenforceable and sometimes even dividends are out of director or management control (stockholders may vote on the payout or policy).

These differences are only the beginning. Even to get to them often requires an understanding of unique and sometimes conflicting local accounting procedures. Specific areas of importance to merger and acquisition analysis relate to reserves depreciation practices, entangling commitments, and expense write-offs.

The meaning of "reserves" in Europe is entirely different from its meaning in the United States. Declared dividends are often close to one hundred percent of the reported income, but this need not be construed as bad policy because an unknown amount of income may have been placed into equally unknown reserve accounts. In bad times, the reserves provide the wherewithall to keep the reported income up. Reserves can be set up for any purpose including devaluation and become a form of undistributed profits. Furthermore, while reserves set aside for such accounts as severance pay are not available to shareholders when the time comes for their ostensibly intended use, they are sometimes insufficient. No explanation may be given and there are no records available for analysis. Sometimes the reserves are funneled off to subsidiaries and, in a sense, are "frozen." But, since the outsider is seldom sure what has happened, evaluation is difficult.

Depreciation practices also vary greatly. Most countries have a maximum allowable rate, but few companies take the maximum. The maintenance of dividends may override a conservative approach to depreciation. Assets may have been underdepreciated for a period of years in order to pay out dividends. In this way, management was indirectly liquidating part of the firm without really acknowledging it. Furthermore, investments in affiliates and subsidiaries are carried on the books as "participators" and could be part of a spider web of hazardous connections. In order to determine the risks that might be involved, it is necessary to check the extent of any debt guarantees. Finally, some costs that American firms would expense immediately are capitalized in some countries and presented with other deferrals. The law of some countries requires that costs associated with research and development, for example, be deferred as assets with the product regardless of the eventual profitability of the product. As can be seen, failure to understand unique accounting practices can be a major stumbling block in valuation.

Most domestic valuation methods rely heavily upon reported earnings, but "earnings" in many foreign enterprises are subject to a wide latitude of interpretation. Even the "generally accepted accounting principles" are changed when you leave the United States. In the United States, the financial statement usually reflects fairly accurately a company's position. In Europe it is merely "in accordance with legal provisions." Many European companies prepare their balance sheets and profit and loss statements to show authorities how little has been made, not to show stockholders how much money has been made. And there are about as many statement forms as there are companies.

Evaluating non-American financial statements is hazardous even for the experts. Different laws and practices can conceal asset or liability valuation, performance data, and even sales data. Subsidiaries' and parent's income do not have to be reported on a consolidated basis. "Fully disclosed, freely available financial reports are the exception rather than rule . . . the extent of disclosure is appalling by United States standards."[5] F. Hoffman LaRoche, for example, recently reported earnings as only fifteen percent of true consolidated earnings and provided no sales or expense figures. The following data was provided by their board of directors:

> The results . . . again show improvement over the year before. Sales and earnings increased in approximately equal proportions. The global development . . . shows a somewhat slower rate of expansion than in previous years but remains at a high level . . . the volume of investment was again large, and will hardly diminish in the foreseeable future. . . .[6]

Such companies as Michelin, Rhone-Poulenc, and Nestle do the same thing. From the analyst's standpoint, such reports lack useful information, comparability, consistency, and acceptability.

Potential Impact on Capital Structure

Perhaps the biggest concern for the acquisition-minded American firm is the impact of a potential subsidiary on the capital structure of the parent. It is afraid to acquire a firm that will not have an immediate, positive impact. The problem, however, is that most foreign firms have much higher debt/equity ratios than do their American counterparts. As discussed in chapter 8, this leverage is often perfectly normal and even good business sense overseas, but it does create problems for the United States multinational.

For one thing, since American firms have consolidated balance sheets, firms acquired overseas often have the net effect of increasing the MNC's debt/equity ratio. If the United States market reacts negatively to such an effect, the price of the MNC's stock could go down and interest rates on future debt issues may go up.

Another problem is encountered in using normal evaluation pro-

[5]Jeffrey S. Arpan, "International Differences in Disclosure Practices, Hazard for Overseas Investment," *Business Horizons* (October 1971), p. 68.

[6]Quoted in *ibid.*

cedures. It is simply not adequate to use the same standards in comparing various firms around the world. Take the practice of evaluating firms on the basis of their returns on equity (ROE). Firms able to operate in countries permitting (sometimes even rewarding) high-leverage positions may be able to show higher returns without having better-run businesses.

The ROE figures can be even more misleading if one is not careful to consider fully all aspects of equity contribution. But this is not an easy matter—especially for outsiders—because the equity base is subject to interpretation and local rules. Capital contributed by minority investors or foreigners may not necessarily be included.

Return on assets (ROA) is a possible alternative ratio to use. It is also a good idea to look at such ratios as: (1) profit on capital employed, (2) profit on sales, (3) profit per employee, (4) sales as a ratio of capital employed, (5) sales to fixed assets, (6) sales to stocks (inventory), and (7) sales to employee.[7] All of these ratios can be useful in analysis, but the most important one is probably the first one; it measures the ability of assets to generate profits.

The usefulness of ROA, unfortunately, is also limited. The basis for evaluation of assets varies. For example, assets are affected by inflation so the use of historical cost figures in an inflationary economy overstates return. Nevertheless, historical cost figures are frequently used because other figures either are not permitted under local accounting rules or are difficult to estimate.

An Overview

We have looked at the pitfalls of acquisition valuation both in the United States context and, more broadly, in the international arena. While many of the criteria used by businessmen in the United States apply overseas, this chapter has identified some of the problems associated with using them. No criteria for analysis has been completely satisfactory.

Several people over the years have tried to develop a universally applicable criteria for valuation. Hodgson and Uyterhoeven have suggested using operating margin analysis (operating margin equals sales minus cost of goods sold) to evaluate overseas opportunities, but the difficulty of estimating expenses and other costs has limited this approach.[8] Furthermore, the popularity of discounted future earnings

---

[7]For a more complete discussion of these ratios, see Anthony Vice, *The Strategy of Takeovers: A Casebook of International Practice* (New York: McGraw-Hill, Inc., 1971), p. 24.

[8]Raphael Hodgson and Hugo Uyterhoeven, "Analyzing Foreign Opportunities," *Harvard Business Review*, March-April 1962, p. 65.

approaches in the United States has also discouraged such a simple, nondiscounting technique.

Most analysts believe that we should use present-value techniques. Gaddis, for example, suggests we find the "*estimated aggregate* of all returns which accrue to the investing company—a *lumped, one probability return* (LOPR)."[9] This will make returns in one situation comparable with returns in another. Gaddis makes three suggestions for "realistic comparisons": (1) An in-depth view of the structure of the projected investment must be made; (2) the acquisition must be applicable to the corporation planning the investment; (3) forecasts must have probability distributions attached to them as indicators of risk. In essence, the company should be looking at the "synergistic" effects of the total investment, that is, the ripple effects that will make the investment, as a whole, greater than the sum of its parts.

The problem with such techniques is that the data used is historical —taken from past records—which brings us back to the same problems mentioned earlier. The data often are suspect (or worse) even if available, and come from various environments having different standards, costs, inflation rates, and accounting systems. If taken at face value, the use of such information could lead to major blunders overseas.

This chapter has reviewed the variables the analyst has to be aware of in order to evaluate acquisitions in an international context. The conclusion must be that the evaluation of potential acquisitions overseas is more difficult because less reliable information is available, accounting and business practices vary, and normal domestic evaluation techniques are often inappropriate or impossible to use. Selective ratio analysis can be of some limited value, and discounted, expected future earnings is sometimes a helpful indicator, but the analyst must be careful. There is no single or simple valuation method which is universally applicable.

---

[9]Paul O. Gaddis, "Analyzing Overseas Investments," *Harvard Business Review*, May-June 1966, p. 116.

Bibliography

Adler, Michael, and Bernard Dumas, "Optimal International Acquisitions." *Journal of Finance*, March 1975, pp. 1–19.

Aharoni, Yair. *The Foreign Investment Decision Process.* Boston: Harvard Graduate School of Business Administration, Division of Research, 1966.

Arpan, Jeffrey S. "International Differences in Disclosure Practices, Hazard for Overseas Investment." *Business Horizons,* October 1971, pp. 67–70.

Cunitz, Jonathan A. "Valuing Potential Acquisitions." *Financial Executive,* April 1971, pp. 20–25.

Gaddis, Paul. "Analyzing Overseas Investments." *Harvard Business Review,* May-June 1966, pp. 115–22.

Grauer, F. L.; R. Litzenberger, and R. Stehle, "Sharing Rules and Equilibrium in an International Capital Market Under Uncertainty." *Journal of Financial Economics,* June 1976, pp. 233–56.

Haner, F. T. "Determining the Feasibility of Foreign Ventures." *Business Horizons,* Fall 1966, pp. 35–44.

Helfert, Erich. *Valuation: Concepts and Practice.* Belmont, Calif.: Wadsworth Publishing Co., 1966.

Hodgson, Raphael, and Hugo Uyterhoeven, "Analyzing Foreign Opportunities." *Harvard Business Review,* March-April 1962, pp. 60–79.

Piper, James. "How U.S. Firms Evaluate Foreign Investment Opportunities." *MSU Business Topics,* Summer 1971, pp. 11–20.

Ricks, David, Marilyn Fu, and Jeffrey Arpan, *International Business Blunders.* Columbus, Ohio: Grid, Inc., 1974.

Robock, Stefan. "It's Good for Growth, But Who's Swallowing?" *Columbia Journal of World Business,* November-December 1967, pp. 13–23.

Tomlinson, James W. *The Joint Venture Process in International Business.* Cambridge, Mass.: M.I.T. Press, 1970.

Van Cise, J. G. "Antitrust Guides to Foreign Acquisition." *Harvard Business Review,* November-December 1972, pp. 82–88.

Vice, Anthony. *The Strategy of Takeovers: A Casebook of International Practice.* New York: McGraw-Hill, Inc., 1971.

INDEX